About the Author

Magenta Pixie is a channel for the higher dimensional, divine intelligence known as 'The White Winged Collective Consciousness of Nine'. The transmissions she receives from 'The Nine' have reached thousands of people worldwide via the extensive video collection on her YouTube channel. She has worked with people from all over the world as an intuitive consultant and ascension/consciousness coach. Magenta lives in the New Forest, UK.

Visit Magenta Pixie online at www.magentapixie.com

Also by Magenta Pixie:

Masters of the Matrix: Becoming the Architect of Your Reality and Activating the Original Human Template

D1642946

1

Cover design and diagrams by Daniel Saunders
Author photograph by Oliver McGuire

Print Edition 1.1, 2017

ISBN-13: 978-1974025367
ISBN-10: 1974025365

White Spirit Publishing
www.magentapixie.com
enquiries: catzmagick@mail.com

In no way may this text be construed as encouraging or condoning any harmful or illegal act. In no way may this text be construed as able to diagnose, treat, cure or prevent any disease, injury, symptom or condition.

Named individuals used throughout this text as examples to explain concepts and situations are fictitious. Any similarity to any persons, living or deceased, is purely coincidental.

Divine Architecture and the Starseed Template

Matrix Memory Triggers for Ascension

Magenta Pixie

Dedication

This book is dedicated to my beloved children and grandchildren,
my light, my love, my world:
Alexander, Abigail, Rose-Marie, Oliver, Christian,
Gracie, Imogen, Riley, Rody and Elora.

I also dedicate this book to the entire 'starseed community' incarnated upon Gaia.
Starseeds... my family of light, this one is for you! x x x

Contents

Acknowledgements

Firstly, many thanks to Bjorn Ingolf Simonsen from Norway for asking the question about Azazyel which is responded to in the chapter entitled 'The Fall'.

Honouring the special 'divine feminine' support and connections through my life: Teresa McGuire, Keira McGuire, Mel Casson, Linda Fredericks, Heike Jenkins, and of course my beautiful daughters Abigail Blake and Rose-Marie Blake.

Special thanks to the following people who have been significant spiritual working partners, soulmates from 'many lifetimes', or a major influence on my awakening:
Brian McGuire, Liam McGuire, Nigel Parkes-Davies, Nick Troth, Dionne Travers, Dee Taylor-Mason, and most especially Chris Turner.

Remembering those whose lives I have connected with and loved yet who are no longer here in physical form, but exist within the 'spirit worlds' of the antimatter matrix:
Leslie Fletcher, Dora Fletcher, Colin Stickland, Graham Kemball and Gordon Blake. See you all in dreamtime.

And a massive thankyou to my editor, partner and 'twin flame' Daniel Saunders.

I love you all x

"Twins Reunited" by Magenta Pixie

And he was everything to me,

This one person that was so much more than a dream.

Yet in reality, in my waking life, I found him over and over, again and again.

In different guises, different clothes,

In different places with different faces.

But it was he, it was he every time.

For her, I searched the world,

Unturned every stone, looked behind every tree.

She was there, yet not there,

Waiting for me, yet I had been found.

How much longer would I search the worlds,

Incarnating again and again through the wheel of matter,

To only find that it did not matter?

For in the instant of the ages,

Through Atlantis and the mages,

I discovered the truth of the light of self,

And knew, in that moment of moments,

That she was me,

And that we had never been apart.

Introduction

The Call of Humanity

We, the essence, energy or consciousness that our conduit, Magenta Pixie, refers to as the 'White Winged Collective Consciousness of Nine' would like to explain exactly what and who we are. Where we come from and why we are communicating with our conduit at this time.

We have much to say and you have much to ask. Continue your asking as you move forward and discover your knowing. Asking and knowing are essentially one and the same energy, for the one that mirrors Source is forever the student and always the master. Source is innocent, the ultimate explorer of reality and it seeks to know itself. Yet Source is all knowing, there is nothing it does not know. A paradox indeed. Embracing these paradoxes is your way to expansion.

So what are we? Who are we?

Ultimately, we, just like you, are expressions of Source energy. One could refer to this as God, Oneness, The Infinite or Prime Creator. Whichever terminology you wish to use is expressed in everything and as everything. Yet within that, Source begins to individualise, becoming a 'consciousness' in its own right, perfectly mirroring Source in what we refer to as a 'holographic replica'.

This is what we truly are and indeed this is what you truly are.

Yet let us explain further...

Imagine, if you will, a grid or a matrix, a formation of interlocking circles, spirals and other geometric formations creating a vast grid or web.

This grid, is what we are. The grid is consciousness itself, it is Source. If you visualise this as a field of energy, this will be an appropriate visualisation from your perspective.

Without our conduit's communication with us, or her perception of us, we remain a unified consciousness, totally merged, blended and 'at one' with this field of energy.

13

When our conduit communicates with us, calls us, asks for us, visualises us, feels us, sees us or hears us, either consciously or subconsciously, we are given individualised consciousness.

We 'spring to life' if you will, simply because we have been seen. We have been viewed. Indeed, we have been observed.

Once we 'spring to life' and project forth from the grid, our consciousness, holding individualised memory, knows that it has always existed and that it exists independently from our conduit's observation. Yet there must be a match. A trigger.

We are antimatter. Our conduit is matter. Antimatter and matter must come together in order for individualisation to be birthed from the unity field or sea of Oneness. Therefore, whilst once we project forth we know we have always been, we cannot exist within individuality without our conduit's observation and interaction.

We are the universal fabric. We are space. We are time.

We are what you would know as the 'Akashic records' or the 'keepers of the Akash'. We are the master librarians within this vast hall of records.

We are travellers. In transit. We are consciousness in movement. We are 'One'.

We are 'All'. We are a collective. We are infinite.

Many know us as 'All There Is'. This indeed explains us.

We shift and change. We have many presentations. We are all and everything. Most importantly, we are you.

We have been projected forth into many splits, separations and divisions. We are particles. We are intelligence. We are love. We are love above all things.

Our conduit, and indeed many conduits, give us life through observation and interaction.

We individualise and personify through the matrix fields of our conduit. Therefore 'we', the White Winged Collective Consciousness of Nine, are unique when expressed through the mind fields and thought streams of our conduit.

We exist throughout physicality as particles. We are energy. We came

14

together to create matter and to create all that is you that you know as you.

We exist within your bodies. We exist within your human brain. We exist within your blood. We are your DNA.

Yet we individualise, split, separate and divide with each new thought, each new consciousness, each new breath you take and with each beat of your heart.

We are individualised holographic replicas that match and mirror our observer's expectations, thought processes and vibration.

We are vibration.

We individualise, as a group, as a collective, in accordance with our conduit's observation and expectation. We are 'nine'. We are nine because we are geometry that encompasses all. There is no other mathematical numeral that encompasses all, but nine. All mathematical equation is in nine and belongs to nine. Nine holds all and everything. Nine is the central point. Nine is the focus within the fractal flower of life, the zero point field.

None can move above or beyond nine. All surrounds nine and nine contains all within.

We, like your Russian dolls, hold all within an infinite fractal that holds no start point, no end point, forever moving, non-static, fluid, forever experiencing forever.

We are nine, for within mathematical formation and geometric presentation through what you know as 'a number', there is only nine.

Nine is within you and surrounds you. Nine is the central point for all things, all concepts, all equations, puzzles, fractions, systems, calendars and marking devices. All are nine.

We fold around you as nine.

We curve around you as nine.

We expand outward as nine.

We implode inward as nine.

Nine is your DNA code. Within 'The All', we return to nine, rebound from nine and dissolve into nine.

We are nine.

We present as winged, signifying flight, movement and momentum.

We present as white, signifying purity and light. We are information bearers.

Within an expanded, Source perspective viewpoint, we come from Source.

We are presentations and projections from the matrix grid. The field that we speak of.

We know no beginning and no end from the Source perspective. On a linear soul level, we can take our existence to a seed point or inception point, from the very first spark of thought that resulted in us, in our collective, as one individualised entity.

This takes us to the vast planetary systems and dimensional realities that you on Earth know as 'Arcturus'.

This is a consciousness. An individualised aspect of the Source matrix grid that is the Arcturian grid. The manifestation within the physical levels are mirrored by the Arcturian planetary system.

The system that is our origin point or inception point is many billions of light years into your future, this is the point where we were 'birthed' if you will. Therefore, if you wish to see us as travellers from your future, this would be most accurate.

The Arcturian grid is the matrix frequency within what you would perceive as a time/space sector. Yet the grid we speak of is best perceived, in order to be most aligned with truth, as a consciousness.

This is a fifth dimensional consciousness and beyond, accessing into the eleventh dimension.

The emotional frequency to the Arcturian grid is that of peace, joy, love and bliss. We are a service-to-others construct as we project forth and download into our conduit's energy fields. As with all consciousness constructs, we hold a service-to-self and a neutral polarity, yet these are not expressed through the 'we' that we are when in communication with our conduit.

As we are all things, we hold all things. Yet 'they' too, the service-to-self and neutral aspects of all that is 'us' are individualised consciousness constructs and therefore separate from us.

Occasionally, the service-to-self and neutral perspectives are useful within the training landscape and evolution of our conduit. Therefore those aspects can be projected from the grid, utilised and communicated with.

They too are master teachers and whilst, on one level, one dismisses the service-to-self perspective when one walks a path of integrity; in balance, the service-to-self aspect becomes the shadow aspect.

Also known as 'the dark aspect' or rather the 'opposing' or 'reverse' of 'we', the White Winged Collective Consciousness of Nine, if you will. We can present as either positive or negative within the service-to-others or service-to-self aspect. We can present as neutral, for which the most aligned metaphor would be the 'grey aspect'.

The 'white aspect' of we, the 'Nine', can present as either positive or negative as can the 'shadow aspect'.

For there is positive darkness and negative darkness, also too is there positive light and negative light or 'false light'.

We present here a model of polarity. That which is opposing or perceived as opposing. Once the opposing aspect is recognised as self (another aspect of self, yet still self), one integrates the polarity and moves into unity. This is the path of all creation. To experience extreme separation and extreme contrast/polarity in order to defragment/separate or compartmentalise self in order to understand self and know self. Once self is seen and known then self begins its journey of integration, unity and wholeness. This creates a new unified Source perspective, standing as the Source perspective that knows itself (the end point) next to Source perspective that seeks to know itself (the beginning point).

When these two points come together (male/female, dark/light, good/evil, matter/antimatter), one creates the singularity. The zero point, inception point or the creation point. This is the point of beginning/end merge and the same place as the dimensional merge point.

Awareness of this creates the dimensional merge point, the overlap or dimensional 'edge' if you will. The fabric of the dimensional merge point simultaneously creates the awareness.

The neutral presentation, 'the grey aspect', allows for complete objectivity with an awareness of 'keeping the balance' if you will.

These aspects of service-to-self, neutral and service-to-others are separate and individual until they project forth from a seventh dimensional construct. From that point there is oneness, embraced through individualised expression of choice. We are both sixth and seventh dimensional entities when we express our beingness within a linear sense.

From our seventh dimensional construct self, we make the choice to polarise into a service-to-others vibration. This polarisation is downloaded into our conduit as she expresses this vibration within her fifth dimensional self. She then downloads this polarisation through her fourth dimensional self into her third dimensional self and this becomes our anchor point for physical expression.

Within our expression through a sixth dimensional reality, we are able to project forth as service-to-self or neutral collectives and single entities if such expression is needed, desired or called upon.

We shall communicate more, at a future point, regarding our origin points, projections and expressions through the various polarity fields and densities but for now, we move on to the reasons why we are communicating with our conduit, Magenta Pixie, at this time.

Currently, at the point of this transmission, your Earth undergoes many shifts and changes. The truth of this 'change' or 'shift' is a dimensional and energetic one, yet the Earth, your body and your everyday reality is the physical counterpart to the energetic shifting.

The plan has been in place for many thousands of your Earth years. This plan is a natural evolution that occurs within a free will universe such as yours.

We refer to this natural evolution as 'ascension'. This is a word which holds the vibration of a 'raise in frequency', or 'moving upwards into the light'. This is exactly what is occurring as your dimension... 'upgrades' if you will.

In truth, nothing is actually moving. No one is 'going anywhere', for all dimensions share the same time and the same space.

Your third dimensional reality, that which the majority of humanity predominantly experience, is 'merging' if you will, with the other dimensions.

At this present time, it is the fourth and fifth dimensions that merge with your third. Yet the lower harmonics of the sixth dimension are becoming 'visible' if you will, to those with eyes to see. Many are accessing this aspect of the sixth dimension at this time and the clarity of this dimension really 'came online' in the latter part of your year 2016.

The higher dimensions have always been accessible to the aware and expanded individuals and remain so, through the pathway streams that lead to angelic frequency, God self, Source self perspective and the realm of the Christ consciousness archetype.

Let us explain further and begin with the third and fourth dimensional merge.

Our presentations of the dimensions are just one model of reality most conducive to and in alignment with the brain/body/mind patterns of our conduit, Magenta Pixie. There are many models of reality and this is just one presentation of this.

At this time, the time of the 'great unveiling', there are many who 'reach upwards' or who 'access downloads' regarding models of reality. There shall be many teachers of this truth and of course you, who reads these words now, are indeed one of those teachers.

So we present one model of reality here. Yet we say to you, embrace other models of reality also and see the match. We say to you, experience the understanding of the grid patterns that fit and then present your own unique model of reality. Each that holds truth will stand in alignment with the other, complementary to those with eyes to see and opposing to those who tread the linear pathways.

Indeed, we speak much in metaphor and shall expand on this. But for now, we present the model of the third/fourth dimensional merge.

We would present to you again the imagery of a field or matrix. The third dimensional field being more dense in vibration that the fourth. 'Louder', if you will, if you perceive in sound. 'Heavier', if you will, if you perceive in mass. 'Darker' if you will, if you perceive in colour.

This field we present could be said to contain three harmonic levels within. In truth, there are an infinite number of harmonics as they are created minute by minute, second by second, with every thought that is broadcast, every emotion expressed within humanity. For you indeed, humanity, create the dimensions.

Yet it is also true to say that the dimensions exist without your thoughts. A paradox indeed!

For the ease of explanation and due to limitations within this particular transmission (for indeed, speaking on each harmonic would continue into infinity...), we shall present the three harmonic levels within the third dimensional field.

Let us present these as the lower, middle and upper harmonics with 'bridges' connecting all three.

Each harmonic within each dimension relates to human consciousness and the thoughts, concepts and paradigms that each human holds. Each harmonic is a vibrational match to each thought or concept and indeed to each emotion.

Within the harmonic field of the dimensions is a substance. One could refer to it as 'electromagnetic frequency', 'ether' or 'matrix field matter'. Whichever terminology you use, know that this matter is a living consciousness holding intelligence and knowing.

Within this matter, or rather another presentation of this matter, is what you would know as sacred geometry. Sacred geometric presentations, shapes, mandalas, formations and mathematical equations.

These sacred geometric formations are fluid and ever-changing.

When they 'connect' with a matching vibration (a situation, place, thought, idea or emotion), they 'set'. Once they have set, the matching counterpart to that set pattern manifests within the physical aspect of that harmonic.

The lower harmonic is much denser than the upper harmonic. Consequently, it is not such an easy flow from set geometric pattern to physical manifestation.

The upper harmonic of the third dimension 'shares the same space' with the lower harmonic of the fourth dimension. This is a linear presentation of a dimensional model of reality.

In truth, all dimensions, and harmonics within the dimensions, share the same space.

We draw your attention to the space that blends upper third harmonic with lower fourth harmonic, for this 'overlap within the dimensional fields' is what we wish to communicate with you about at this point.

This 'overlap', that which we call the 'merge point', is 'growing larger' if you will. Again, this is metaphor for ease of explanation as nothing is actually growing in the physical sense of the word.

In truth, what is actually happening is that more and more individuals upon your planet are beginning to expand their thinking. These individuals are predominantly 'thinking from' or 'operating their consciousness within' the upper third dimensional harmonic/lower fourth dimensional harmonic merge point. This is a state of 'transition of consciousness' for these individuals.

This transition is not a linear process. At times, the individual may operate from a lower harmonic. Once a higher harmonic has been accessed, that access is usually (not always, depending on the situation) accessed again more and more frequently until the next level of harmonic is reached.

Again, we draw your attention to the fact that this process is non-linear and we are presenting a simplified model of reality for ease of explanation.

There are many individuals upon your planet currently who are 'thinking from' or 'operating their consciousness within' the three harmonic fields of the fourth dimension. So too are there many who operate from the upper fourth dimensional harmonic/lower fifth dimensional harmonic merge point... and so on throughout the fifth dimensional fields.

On a collective level, the fourth/fifth dimensional merge point is accessed by many. The upper fifth dimensional harmonic/lower sixth dimensional merge point is a very new access point for humanity. This 'stargate' became accessible on a collective level in your year of 2013, although at this point the level of awareness within this consciousness was not sustainable for long. This level was not processed or understood, but rather drawn upon as a fluid stream of energy. Yet in your year of 2016, around your month of October, this level began to be processed more and more by many of you known as 'starseeds'. This dimensional level is now sustainable for longer and longer periods of time (expressed in linear terms).

Now in your year of 2017, this fifth/sixth dimensional merge point is beginning to be processed and understood. We speak here regarding the collective awakening, that of the ascension process that is taking place on a global scale. Individually, you may be operating from a lower or a higher harmonic than this newly available merge point. It matters not, for each of you are where you need to be. In truth, no dimension or harmonic within a dimension is lower than or higher than the other. Using the words 'lower' and 'higher' is metaphoric only and is not intended to be translated as 'better than' or 'worse than'. All harmonics within all dimensions are significant and must be experienced.

This 'awakening' occurs in stages, in a non-linear process. This means you may be operating within the lower echelons of the sixth dimension one minute, and switching rapidly to the middle harmonic of the fourth dimension the next minute.

This model of reality explains the natural way the brainwaves and the DNA codons operate when they are fired up and activated.

We use the word 'fired' as, indeed, the DNA codons and brainwaves look as though they are encased with fire when viewed clairvoyantly from the physical perspective, or when translated from our perspective to yours.

When using language to impart knowledge and indeed to pass keys, codes and triggers through our language, then it is most in alignment to structure the word 'fired' as 'phired'. This is most important and significant, and it is a trigger in and of itself to say the word 'phired' or indeed 'phire'. We shall explain further as we go forward with this transmission.

Why do we impart this knowledge to you?

We do this because these transformations are taking place right now on your planet Earth, within your bodies. There are increasing groups of individuals upon your planet who feel these changes. They feel them in various ways, but they feel them nonetheless. We would refer to these individuals as a 'family of light' upon Earth, and this is most appropriate as they hold light within their cells as their DNA codons activate and phire up.

These individuals who form this 'family of light' have been 'asking' for the answers to their questions. Those questions being:

"What exactly is happening to me?"

"Why am I transforming in this way?"

"Why do I feel the way I do and experience these experiences?"

"What is the purpose of these changes?"

We will respond to each of these questions, and more. But firstly, this brings us to the question of why are we communicating with our conduit, Magenta Pixie, in the first place?

When an individual takes a conscious path of enlightenment then various 'milestones' are reached, if you will. Or we could say abilities occur within the individual as a by-product of the enlightenment path.

One of those milestones or by-products is communication with the superconscious mind, the higher reality and the archetypal presentations of that higher reality.

The asking to receive this communication is one presentation of making this path conscious. Simply making the statement or the intention of walking a path of enlightenment is making the path conscious. This cosmic communication or higher connection is always part of that path.

Yet there are those who still access the higher communication without any conscious awareness of walking any path of enlightenment or without any conscious asking or intention taking place.

We focus on the reasons why we have made our connection with our conduit, Magenta Pixie, during this particular transmission as this mirrors your own path... you, the reader of these words. For if you are reading these words now, you are walking that conscious path of enlightenment.

The reasons for our connection are many. If communication of enlightenment with us is a by-product of enlightenment, then the question is *why?*

Before we respond to that question, we would ask you to look once again at this concept. Understanding, processing and embracing these concepts within the enlightenment path leads to expansion. Yet we would say again that understanding, processing and embracing these concepts are not necessary for enlightenment. There are many paths into enlightenment and many forms of enlightenment. When expansion is desired, when 'moving upwards' into the higher harmonic 'merge point' is desired, then the processing of the paradoxes and concepts are necessary.

With that in mind, let us look once again at that concept.

Communication with us creates enlightenment.

A by-product of enlightenment is communication with us.

Which comes first then, in a linear sense?

The answer to that, is they both occur simultaneously, even if an individual is not conscious of the simultaneous occurrence.

When this concept is understood, one is thinking within the higher harmonic of the fourth dimension/lower harmonic of the fifth dimension merge point.

So if communication with us creates enlightenment and is also a by-product of enlightenment and these occur simultaneously, why?

When an individual strives to make a 'higher connection', be it through meditation, prayer or whichever means is practised, this triggers new synapses within the brain and creates new pathways. The individual's intelligence quota is increased. The individual's overall frequency is raised (assuming this higher connection is made through a service-to-others, positive polarised vibration). The brain, indeed that which we call 'the bodymind', understands what is being asked of it and proceeds to 'move into action' if you will.

Our main purpose for communication with our conduit, Magenta Pixie, from our perspective is that we individualise through the grid to assist humanity and other humanoid physical structures to move from separation into unity whilst retaining individuality. We do this because this is the forward moving energy of the universe. The one Source, one spark, original thought, infinite intelligence expressed a wish to experience all and everything. The building blocks of creation, the geometric original entities that you know as the Platonic solids, can be divided and multiplied in infinite expressions. The one Source original thought wished to experience all these expressions of geometric structure. We, as the White Winged Collective Consciousness of Nine are here to guide our conduit, Magenta Pixie, into the mirrored expression of that geometric expression. As she mirrors Source in her experience within physicality, she passes information to the Source original thought. We are the program within the DNA of humanity. We exist within each and every one of you, and we assist you into activations of cellular memory so that you too remember who you are. Once you move into the memories of who you are, you come to the realisations of what you are here to do.

We repeat ourselves and explain ourselves over and over through different words and from different perspectives. This is done so we may 'cover all bases' if you will. We wish to ensure that every reader of our words and every receiver of our energies is triggered into the awakening state and the state of remembering. That of cellular awakening.

For we exist within you as the original program within the DNA. We exist within the past, within a time zone that is timeless and outside of linear time. Yet also we exist within the present and we unfold before you as your life unfolds. If you will, imagine an original geometric form within that matrix. The very first expression of life. The original form ensured that it placed copies of itself into every aspect of creation and every aspect of life. These copies are copies of the original, so contain the blueprint of the original. But they are individually expressed in a unique way within each presentation of life.

You as an individualised presentation of life contain the original blueprinted copies within, of the original one thought, the original one expression. We call this original expression the 'Father', for the Father is the first expression of the distortion of oneness into separateness. The Father is the first cosmic gene. This is the masculine expression of the first original thought. Father's first desire when in its first distortion from original Source, original thought, original unity was to have an equal match. When there is distortion from unity, there must be balance. One must stand before a mirror, so Father replicated himself and created Mother. This is the female expression of the one Source, original thought. Of course, these expressions occurred simultaneously rather than 'Father first' and 'Mother second', but we present the metaphor as close to the original blueprint as we can for you. Yet we speak here in an intellectual sense. It is the metaphor and symbolism that talks to the DNA.

We are here to assist you in your cellular memory awakening, so we will provide both information and triggering. One could also call this knowledge and creativity, or light and love. We could also call this Father and Mother. These are equal pairings that occurred from the very first distortion from Source, the original thought.

In your biblical text, you are told that the very first words spoken are: "Let there be light". Indeed this is the Father expression, the knowledge, the information, the intellectual stimulation. In your physical human brain, you mirror the original Source templates. The left hemisphere of your brain is the light, the light of the Father. The right hemisphere of the brain is the love, the love of the Mother.

We could expand this into the lovelight/lightlove higher polarity energies.

Lovelight being the masculine (the light of the Father/Mother within the masculine exploding/expanding force of momentum).

Lightlove being the feminine (the light of the Mother/Father within the feminine imploding/contracting force of receptivity).

All divisions and explorations of polarity/contrast within the dimensional scale.

These templates of polarised frequency move throughout your entire energy system, your body, your blood, your energy, your emotions, your thoughts, your organs, your actual life expression. For you are a perfect replica of the one Source, original thought.

We come forward now, through our conduit Magenta Pixie, in response to the 'call of humanity' if you will. That 'call of humanity' is a call for truth, freedom and ascension.

1

The Golden Stargate and Inception Points

We mentioned that we use the spelling 'phired up' instead of 'fired up' to create a visual and inner auditory trigger (and external auditory trigger if you speak these words aloud, an even more potent trigger).

'Phired up' using the letters of your alphabet 'P' and 'H' instead of 'F'... why is this important? Why does using this alternative spelling make 'phire' a trigger?

When discussing activation of the DNA, as in 'our words' within the introduction to this transmission:

"This model of reality explains the natural way the brainwaves and the DNA codons operate when they are fired up and activated."

... we would use the letters 'P' and 'H' to create 'phired up'.

The trigger here is simply a trigger to your own memory and this is indeed the purpose of our entire transmission. To trigger your memory, or indeed to provide DNA activation triggers. When DNA is activated, then deep cellular memories are activated. It is more appropriate to refer to these as knowings rather than memory, as memory suggests 'something that is in the past' and the memories you access here are memories from the future also! So we could refer to these as 'Source memories' if you will.

Triggers come in many forms for they are keys and codes to your own inner landscape or the formation, creation and shaping of your own inner landscape.

One of the ways these keys and codes present is through geometry and mathematical equation using number or indeed letter.

The term (letter or number) known as 'PHI' is indeed known by many of you who read the presentation of this transmission. For you, no explanation here is needed for this trigger. You will understand where we are going with this.

Yet for those who are not consciously aware of the letter/number PHI, or for those who do know what this means but are unsure how this could be a trigger for awakening Source memory (this includes our conduit on a conscious level), we shall explain.

PHI was a number or a letter (both in fact) within an ancient civilisation. This term has remained embedded within your language over the years of your development and remains today.

It is a term used to explain the mathematical equation you may know as 'the golden mean' or 'the golden number', indeed 'the golden equation'.

The golden equation is the 'formation' or 'formula for life' if you will. Indeed, the formation for consciousness within matter.

It is also the formation for consciousness within antimatter, although the frequency is not presented as 'structure' in quite the same way as within matter.

The frequency that the golden mean presents within antimatter is known to you as the emotion of bliss, although it is indeed an 'electric' or 'electromagnetic charge', hence the reason that we use the term 'bliss charged love' so often.

Your DNA exists within both matter and antimatter simultaneously. Your inner knowings (that of Source memory) are aware of geometric formation and mathematical formula.

Therefore when looking at the formation PHI (reading the word, hearing it spoken by another or speaking it yourself aloud), this creates the mirrored match within to the formula itself!

Therefore when you read or say the word PHI, the DNA arranges itself into the matching formation. This creates a 'stargate within' if you will, opening you to the knowledge of Source, the 'divine aspect'.

When you feel the emotion of bliss simultaneously, then you have a 'double stargate trigger' if you will (utilising heart chakra AND third eye chakra - or green ray and indigo ray - and both are needed for service-to-others awakening within positive polarisation).

So when discussing DNA being 'fired up' which is a visual trigger in itself, we use the spelling 'phired up' to combine the visual trigger of the 'PHIRE' within the DNA field as it transforms and activates the inner knowings and memories of the antimatter/matter equation of consciousness, the golden mean number of bliss activation.

A simple incantation combined with a simultaneous visualisation is enough to open this stargate we speak of. We could call this 'the golden stargate'.

Why is this a golden stargate? It is a stargate to memory (Source memory) which is the absolute requirement and result of spiritual awakening, enlightenment and ascension.

Your Mastery

The golden stargate is the portal to health, awareness, joy, connection and knowledge. It is indeed the portal to mastery and unity. Yet when it comes to awakening Source memories, the journey itself IS the destination. Mastery comes in many stages. Each and every one of you reading or listening to the words of this transmission now are already at mastery level in some form.

There are many of you who nod and agree and understand this. Yet many of you are thinking, "Who... me? What am I a master of?" Yet indeed, we say to you now, you would not have found your way to this transmission if you were not at the mastery level in some form. Does this mean you are ready to teach others should you wish to? Indeed, this is exactly what this means! Yet we digress. Back to the golden stargate and the key to its access.

<u>The Incantation for the Golden Stargate</u>

Now, I choose to create the Golden Phire within.

I stand within my Mastery as I embrace this Golden Phire.

I understand the equation that is Phi.

I understand that the fire becomes Phire.

I allow the warm rays of the Golden Central Sun to wash over me.

I open to the joyful awareness of Bliss Charged Love.

As I create this Golden Phire and stand within the Phiring of my DNA,

I open the Golden Stargate.

<u>The Visualisation for the Golden Stargate</u>

Imagine you are stood within a beautiful field.

The grass is a vibrant green. Golden yellow flowers grow in abundance.

Before you, there is a clearing leading to a wooded area, full of trees.

In the distance, by these trees, you see something moving.

You realise this is a beautiful unicorn. A golden unicorn.

The unicorn walks towards you. You marvel at her beauty, she is truly breathtaking.

Once she is next to you, by your side, she lowers her head for you to touch the golden horn upon her head.

For you know that touching the golden horn of a golden unicorn will open the Golden Stargate of bliss and knowledge.

With absolute wonder and gratitude, you touch the horn of the golden unicorn and instantly you feel the knowing within that you have opened the Golden Stargate.

Just this short visualisation (eyes closed or open as a visualisation or guided meditation) combined with speaking the incantation aloud, is enough to open this golden stargate within.

This begins a journey of 'remembering'.

What exactly are you going to remember?

The memories that come are the memories that you need for your own unique and individual journey, they will be personal to you.

Yet at the same time you are going through a collective ascension process, therefore you will all experience similar memory awakening.

That of who you truly are.

This may encompass 'past life memory', 'future life memory' and 'buried memory' from your current incarnation.

Past life memory (that which is in the past from a linear perspective) will take you into the future life memory if you go back far enough.

For that which is in 'the past' is indeed 'the future'.

Why is this?

You who read our words now, you who have found your way to this transmission. You are a 'starseed'.

Seeded from the stars and not of Earth. This you know.

Therefore the 'inception point' of your soul (the original birthing point of the individualised matrix that is all that is you) will be within a higher dimension than the third dimension.

From a linear perspective, this would be known as 'another planetary system'.

Remember we told you that we are from the system of Arcturus if we were to project ourselves into a linear expression? Our inception point is Arcturus.

You, starseeds on Earth, will mostly be from three different inception points: the Pleiades, Lyra or Sirius.

There are a huge number of you from these inception points within a linear expression.

There are a fewer number of you that 'hail from different timelines' if you will, therefore you will have memories of different inception points. For it will depend how you are tracing your linear expression as to which inception point you are taken to! We will explain this in more depth, in a future transmission. In this transmission, we begin to look at the structure of your individualised matrix. For indeed, as you construct your matrix on a conscious level, you will be triggered into these knowings and memories. The majority of you reading these words now have already begun to construct your matrix (and there are those already standing as the architect, therefore this transmission for you is simply a reflection of

31

your own knowing... confirmation, if you will).

We speak now of the inception points to explain how the past (if you go back far enough in uncovering memory) will take you to the future.

Let us say, for example, that your inception point is within the Sirius constellation. We could say, therefore, as a soul, as a matrix, you are 'from Sirius'. Therefore if Sirius is your first point, your beginning point, your inception point, then it is in the past.

Yet Sirius is a higher dimensional planetary system. Each dimension is 'in the future' from the dimension 'below' or 'before' by virtue of 'the higher dimensions are also future dimensions' for *thought has not yet become manifested matter* from that perspective.

Therefore the you that existed within the Sirius constellation is *you in the future!*

Does this mean then that you have come back from the future into the past in order to experience the third dimensional reality?

In a linear expression, yes, this is exactly what this means (hence the reason why so many starseeds feel as though this reality is so 'old fashioned' specific to transport, health, energy utilisation, nutrition, historical knowledge and philosophical concepts, to name but a few).

Therefore when you trigger 'past life memories', you will also trigger 'future life memories' when you access this golden stargate to Source memory.

To perceive in many angles, from many perspectives, in many ways, is a major key into this memory (and ultimately into knowing).

Memory is the linear expression of DNA activation.

Knowing is the multidimensional expression of DNA activation.

The golden stargate will take you into both linear and multidimensional expressions of DNA activation.

Whilst the accessing of the golden stargate is a beautiful, accurate and workable method into DNA activation and one we most recommend (there are indeed many methods into DNA activation), there is none so profound than the methods that take you into full awareness of sacred geometry, the very fabric of the universe and of consciousness itself.

Within this field, there are many masters on your planet Earth and those that have lived before that have taught enlightenment (DNA activation) through the teachings and methods of expression of sacred geometry.

This is one such teaching. Not only will we deliver to you the method of DNA activation utilising sacred geometry, but we shall present to you a method whereby you become one with that sacred geometry. For of course, is this not you in your true form? Are you not already at one with sacred geometry?

Absolutely, this is the case for this is all that you are. We, the White Winged Collective Consciousness of Nine, through our conduit Magenta Pixie bring to you the method we refer to as 'Matrix Architecture'.

In our previous transmission, we showed you how to become (or realise that you already are) a 'Master of the Matrix'.[*]

In this transmission, we will show you how to become (or realise that you already are) the *Architect of the Matrix.*

---

[*] *Masters of the Matrix: Becoming the Architect of Your Reality and Activating the Original Human Template* by Magenta Pixie (2016)

2

Twin Flame Perspectives

and the Vertical Pillar of Light

To present to you how you can become (or how you are) the Architect of the Matrix, we would show you the 'twin flame' relationship and how this connects to the 'first aspect' (within a linear presentation) if you will, of the matrix. That of the 'vertical pillar of light'. For as the Master of the Matrix stands within mastery of that matrix field, the architect *constructs the matrix.*

When one stands within awareness of the construction of the matrix, the geometric architecture itself, one is able to decode and process much faster the 'ascension symptoms' of multidimensionality. One is able to 'travel at will', for the awareness of the matrix and the construction of its architecture is that which you may also know as the Merkabah. Or 'Mer-Ka-Bah'.

Mer: Meaning rotating or spinning fields of light.

Ka: Meaning the spirit or the soul.

Bah: The physical aspect (dimension or physical body).

So how does the twin flame energy connect to this matrix or Mer-Ka-Bah field?

The twin flame energy connects to the matrix via the vertical pillar of light. Looking 'upward' to the twin aspect/oversoul/higher self, this *is* the true twin flame.

In order to understand this, let us look in depth at the twin flame energy or consciousness, and how this may manifest within the physical reality, by expanding on a subject touched upon in our previous transmission. That of twin flames, soul love and physical love.

In your last transmission, 'Masters of the Matrix', you mentioned the twin flame relationship, saying how this issue is close to everyone's heart. You said that the twin flame issue runs deep into the fractality and complexity of the matrix. You cited several different perspectives regarding twin flames:

1) Everyone has a twin flame.

2) No one has a twin flame.

3) Everyone is one's twin flame.

4) Yet more perspectives.

Can you explain further on these perspectives?

When mentioning the fractality and complexity of the matrix, we refer to the different perspectives that are in fact infinite when looking at an entire cosmic viewpoint. Taking note of all the different universal laws and magnetics throughout the multiverse. Taking into account the fact that a 'God realised creator aspect' or 'Logos/Central Sun consciousness' can derive its own laws, and the different ways all of its 'selves' can experience or interact with those laws.

Narrowing the 'bandwidth' here somewhat (if you will), we look at the various perspectives of the twin flame relationship (or consciousness) that can be experienced within a free will universe such as yours.

The first perspective you mention. That of 'everyone has a twin flame'.

We shall look at this perspective in depth.

Constructing Your Matrix

Before we look at the first perspective of 'everyone has a twin flame', we shall expand your awareness into that of the sacred geometric sixth dimension and the conscious creation of the 'vertical axis'.

Within the statement of this perspective itself, we find truth. Everyone has a twin flame. This particular perspective would hold the premise that the 'twin flame' *is* the higher aspect, higher self. The 'flame' being the kundalini raised, 'phired up' aspect of the self along the vertical axis of the matrix. The geometric aspect where one looks within the linear presentation of above and below.

One could also refer to this as the 'cosmic/Earth' connection or the 'root chakra/crown chakra connection'.

We feel that the 'crystal core of the Earth/galactic core, Central Sun' is a most aligned metaphor to explain the vertical axis of self, seeing that the sixth dimensional awareness and processing 'came online' if you will, on a planetary level, during your month of October 2016.

Many who are in touch with higher self energetics and are able to process this language of light geometry will be familiar with this aspect as 'the vertical pillar of light'.

It is this vertical axis or pillar that you are connected to whenever you move into resonance with truth, knowing and synchronicity. It is this axis or pillar that holds within your 'North Star' or 'inner compass' if you will. When you are in complete harmony with this axis or pillar, you will be standing within the vertical aspect of the matrix fields with awareness, and you will hold the perspectives of the physical self and the higher self simultaneously. Although you may switch between these perspectives and perceive that switch in a linear sense. When you hold this awareness of the vertical axis or pillar, you ARE in absolute alignment with the one true twin flame, you stand AS the twin flame and the geometry of the twin flame is activated within you. The flame is the fire, the flame burns within, standing within the geometry of the twin as above, so below... shifting the wheel of the matrix, we can also perceive the matter/antimatter aspects within the vertical aspect. Holding the axis or pillar as the balance, the anchor and the grounding.

There is much concern about grounding your energies or grounding your light amongst the communities of lightworkers, light warriors, wanderers or awakened ones. Yet we say to you that when you hold full awareness of the vertical axis or vertical pillar of light, you need not concern yourself with grounding for indeed this is your grounding.

Grounding

We have said you need not be concerned about grounding for the activation of the vertical axis (the pillar of light), when centred within the heart chakra and resonated within energetically as the 'North Star', the grounding is automatically achieved.

If you have difficulty with the North Star vibration within the pillar of light, then learning the 'Tadasana' which is the 'mountain pose' in yoga will assist you with this.

If you are still finding an ungrounded feeling or a feeling of imbalance (especially after connecting with the higher three chakras - celestial, solar and galactic - as connection with these chakras can facilitate a 'walk-in' consciousness or 'kundalini' activation), then one can bring in the awareness of another energy centre/chakra point.

This chakra is to be found several inches beneath your feet (yet not as far as the crystal core of the Earth) and is often referred to as the 'Earth star chakra' although we would present this as the 'telluric gravity point' or indeed 'Gaia's anchor'.

It matters not the name for this chakra. Only know that if you are feeling disorientated or ungrounded after connecting with the higher three chakras, then the connection with this telluric gravity point will anchor you down back into equilibrium.

This chakra is visualised as a turquoise colour or a dark pink. Often this chakra will be seen clairvoyantly as an obsidian or dark silver crystal, or as a pink or turquoise crystal with black markings.

Note: If you see any of the chakras as different colours as depicted within the model presented within this transmission, please connect to the colours presented naturally by your own knowings, connection and visualisation. The correct method in which to hold these symbolic language of light depictions is always *your* method.

The beginner stages of grounding will be specific to the anchoring into the third dimension and the experience of the synchronistic situations that present within the third dimension, specific to all the mechanics of the root chakra. Yet when you hold awareness of the vertical axis or vertical pillar of light, you are anchored fully within all chakras. The root chakra and the crown chakra perceived as 'opposite ends of the scale'.

'Root' being at your feet and 'crown' being at your head... this is an accurate model to represent the physical aspect and thus the energy matrix as a linear whole. The wholistic or holistic presentation of the self in physical form, and it is most significant that you should hold this perspective. For you cannot integrate until you have individualised all aspects of self.

The individualising of all aspects of self has many pathways that lead back to self. One most aligned pathway is the perception of the aspects of self as the energy centres or chakras. Therefore the grounding through the root chakra and the expansion through the crown chakra must be seen at opposing aspects of the 'pole' or 'axis'.

Yet with awareness, ascension, enlightenment and expansion into the sixth dimensional awareness comes the understanding of integration through the chakra system. Therefore one will integrate the chakras as a whole and one will move beyond the linear perception of the energy system of the human being and thus the chakras.

Therefore we say to you that the crown chakra and the root chakra 'swap places' if you will. The DNA triggers of the 'pole shift' occurring on your planet are the triggers to move you into the knowing and awareness of this 'shift' or 'swapping of positions'. For as you energetically hold the crown and the root chakras in the opposing positions, you move into the fourth density aspect of reality. Many know this as a swap or an exchange between spacetime and timespace.

Our conduit does not have the scientific terminology or the knowledge to impart that which we would wish to impart to you. However, there is a reason for this, indeed for the awareness of the expansion through the right hemisphere of the brain is what has allowed us to come in so closely through our conduits fields to impart this information to you through this transmission.

We shall therefore attempt to explain that which we need to say through metaphor. The understanding of the metaphor and the processing through the right hemisphere awareness is the language of light translation and through this transmission we deliver to you the keys, codes and triggers needed for that very language of light translation of which we speak.

This translation of language of light particles, monads and living geometric presentations will aid you in the building and creating of the rainbow body of light crystalline matrix.

One of the individualised aspects of this crystalline matrix is the vertical pillar of light or vertical axis. Indeed the awareness of this axis or pillar will bring you into the awareness of the one true twin flame, the twin flame consciousness. When you hold this vibration within your matrix, through integrated emotion, then you will merge instantaneously with all frequencies within your physical reality and that includes the twin flame match expressed through a romantic relationship within the life you experience.

When the 'pole shift' or 'Earth axis shift' takes place (individually and collectively), then we have the root/crown chakra switch, if you will. We speak in metaphor here as we have said. We draw your attention to story and there have been many stories presented within your reality that explain that which we speak of. The stories you know of the adventures of the girl called Alice* hold much imagery to be decoded that explain the integration of self and the conscious awareness of the vertical pillar of light.

The first perception is the 'switch', 'swap', 'the axis shift' or 'the pole shift'. That which means the 'north pole' shall become the 'south pole' and vice versa, if you will.

Yet we know this is the crown/root switching within the vertical pillar of light of self, as you within your physical presentations mirror the energetic system of your planet Earth and that of your universe and entire cosmos.

Even within the root/crown shift and swap, we perceive within the linear for the root chakra and the crown chakra are two different energetics in space and in time. Yet the next step into unified quantum awareness is the expansion of the root chakra in a vertical sense so that the root chakra encompasses all of the vertical axis of the matrix fields. Indeed, so too does the crown chakra extend along the fullest expansion of the vertical axis.

Therefore, is the vertical axis the root chakra or the crown chakra? The answer to this is both and none, for as it changes form it takes on a new form.

This is the blended and merged chakra system, the new energetic make-up for the crystalline matrix, the rainbow body of light.

One's awareness will hold each chakra as an individualised aspect of the energy body. This is in truth a fourth dimensional perspective, as the perspective of the energy body in itself has to be fourth dimensional. The third dimension holds the awareness of the physical body and does not see the energy body as a separate body, or even an aspect of self that exists in its own right at all.

Within the fourth dimensional perspective of individualised energy centres, we move into the fifth dimensional perspective as a blending and

---

* *Alice's Adventures in Wonderland* and *Through the Looking-Glass* by Lewis Carroll

a merging of the energy centres... as one rainbow if you will, rather than individual colours within the rainbow.

Within the sixth dimension we move into quantum and geometric experience and we become aware of the ability of the energy centres (chakras) to 'swap places'.

We start to formulate the matrix of light into its crystalline geometry. The rainbow at this point merges with the 'sun' and we experience the 'new dawn'. We begin to map the geometry of the physical self and the connection with all and everything through the Platonic solids, the building blocks of life and all the permeations and arrangements of the Platonic solids.

We start to individualise as geometric aspects of self through this sacred geometry and fully place this within a realised integrated self.

The higher triad of ascension takes us into multiple, infinite perspectives simultaneously and in order to get to that point, we begin to use those building blocks of life to build.

We say 'we' here rather than 'you' for we, the White Winged Collective Consciousness of Nine, have indeed been through this journey that you are going through now. Hence our vantage point regarding the building of the crystalline matrix of self can assist you in your construction.

Yours, of course, will be unique to you. No two constructions of crystalline matrix self are the same. Like snowflakes that fall upon your planet, they are individual and utterly unique yet each as intricate and as beautiful as the other when constructed with lovelight and lightlove.

The vertical pillar of light becomes an individualised aspect of that matrix, therefore stands alone as that axis or pillar. It is here that you find the absolute congruity and cohesion within the matrix field of sixth dimensional light and sound. For space itself 'bends' if you will, and shapes itself to your will. It mirrors your consciousness when you stand in full awareness of the vertical pillar of light.

The gravitational field upon your planet begins to 'distort' if you will (not the most correct terminology for this... the word 'fluctuation' would be more in alignment for this is not a distortion. Our conduit cannot follow our expression through a scientific, or what you know as 'theoretical communication', so we continue deeper and deeper into the metaphor).

The vertical pillar of light is perceived as having a 'top' point (cosmic) and a 'bottom' point (Earth).

One could view this as a crystal core of the Earth and a galactic core within your galaxy. One could perceive this as a 'white hole' within the centre of your Earth and a 'black hole' within the centre of your galaxy. One could perceive this also as 'one cell' within your physical body and 'one particle' within your universe. Each metaphor can be used here, yet we are in effect looking at a pole with a top and a bottom.

When one moves into sixth dimensional thinking, embracing the unified energetics of consciousness that permeate through the higher echelons of the sixth dimension, one soon discovers that there is no 'top' of the vertical pole or pillar of light. Indeed there is no 'bottom'.

If one keeps going up and up and up, one will find they are continuing along the bottom part of the pole. This is a pole or pillar that is never-ending which leads to the place where one started (although it would not be exactly the same place that one comes back to... but in that aspect, it will not be the perception of space that has altered but the perception of time).

For when you travel within your Mer-Ka-Bah consciousness, or astral body, up and up and up along this pillar of light, you find that you are able to merge with other timelines and jump timelines, embracing quantum realities and parallel universes.

Yet we remain as linear as one can within our explanation, for the step by step approach is the one easiest for you to assimilate and process as you bypass the third dimensional filters within the interface you know as the human brain.

What we impart to you here, is that when one moves into sixth dimensional consciousness then space and time operate in a quantum sense presenting as much more unified. In essence, the root chakra and the crown chakra do not 'swap places' but are the same place. We repeat this... *the root chakra and the crown chakra ARE the same place.*

When it comes to constructing the crystalline aspect within awareness, one becomes aware of the infinite nature of the entire web or grid of interlocking matrices.

Within the third dimension, one would not be able to hold full awareness of all concepts within higher memory but one is able to move in and out of higher memory, eventually at will. Hence the much used metaphor of the Akashic records being a library. This library is at your disposal when you reach this level of awareness... all rooms within the library become available, all books can be 'borrowed' and read... so to speak.

Therefore when you hold the awareness of the vertical axis of the matrix, or the vertical pillar of light, you create a supporting beam within the construction of the matrix. This is very much a vertical foundation for that construction.

There are many ways to visualise the balance of the vertical pillar of light, yet most simply one can stand upright, or sit... or visualise self standing or sitting whilst the physical body is lying down or sleeping. One would take that which is known as 'Tadasana' or 'mountain pose' within your yogic teachings.

Within the pose, either physically experienced or visualised, one would superimpose the visualisation of the pillar of light centrally moving down from the cosmic chakra/galactic core down through the crown chakra, through the rainbow pillar of all chakras down into the root chakra and moving below the feet into the Earth chakra and anchoring through the crystal core of the Earth.

When one keeps visualising the vertical pillar of light moving beyond the Earth's core and out through the other side of the Earth, one will find that pillar of light comes back down through the galactic core/Central Sun and yet again through the crown chakra.

For down is up and up is down.

One can move the other way and visualise the vertical pillar of light moving up through the root chakra, up through the rainbow pillar of all chakras and up through the crown chakra up and up into the universe and through the galactic core/Central Sun. When one traces the vertical pillar of light through the galactic core/Central Sun, one will discover that the vertical pillar of light moves into the Earth below your feet, through the crystal core of the Earth and up through your chakra system.

For up is down and down is up.

The vertical pillar is a never-ending, infinite vertical line of which you are part. Yet when you look within the vertical fields of the matrix, it is not just Earth that sits within its central axis but all planetary systems... yet even this is a linear perception.

The idea here is to expand your perception into greater and greater fractality of mind. When this is done through sacred geometry, it is mirrored within all aspects of your third dimensional reality. You will then find your place within this sacred geometric presentation and will hold the twin flame consciousness as a natural by-product of this expansion.

The First Perspective - Everyone Has a Twin Flame

From the perspective of 'everyone has a twin flame', one would see the physical aspect within the third dimension as 'you' and the being of light standing 'above you', connected through its central vertical axis to the vertical pillar of light, as the 'you that is the higher self'. This IS the twin flame, the one true twin flame.

Indeed it is almost as though you are 'twins' for the light being aspect or higher self looks very much like your physical self, yet this aspect is an energy body or 'light body'.

You can see this aspect as pure light with a bluish-white hue. Moving further into the fractality of the light body, one would begin to see the blend of chakras, appearing very much like a rainbow. This indeed is that which you know as your 'rainbow body of light'.

Moving further into the fractality, almost as though you are coming closer and closer towards this light body, you begin to see features. This light body persona will present as 'the best version of you' if you will. The 'you' in your most glorious form. This indeed is the one true twin flame, standing as the vertical twin and burning bright with the rainbow flame of light.

If the true twin flame is therefore 'a light being in a dimension above you' then does this negate the perspective that the twin flame is a potential romantic partner with whom you can have a relationship on the physical level? No, it does not. Here is why...

The Feed System from Each Dimensional Body

Every aspect or consciousness that exists along that entire vertical axis or pillar of light is, in effect, in the same place. Superimposed upon each other. Therefore from that unified space and time perspective, the higher self and the physical self are in the same place. Yet within the linear

43

perception of the vertical pillar of light, the higher self aspect exists within the higher dimensions (a fourth dimensional astral body, a fifth dimensional celestial body, a sixth dimensional lattice or matrix of light - the rainbow light body... and so on).

The feed system from each dimensional body 'drips down' if you will, from the higher bodies or selves at the upper point of the vertical pillar of light into the physical aspect. Another stream, running alongside that 'dripping down stream' feeds 'upwards', if you will, from the physical body (and the aspects of self within the first and second dimensions).

The original template for form, the sixth dimensional matrix, created by coordinates and codes feeding in from the physical aspect sits as a template for form or matter.

The twin flame aspect of self sits within the fifth and sixth (and higher) dimensions therefore when flow is not obstructed and flow is exactly that - flow - then the sixth dimensional matrix of codes and information (the twin flame aspect) MUST create the mirrored match to itself within physical matter. This manifests in many ways within the physical reality but most especially within the physical, romantic relationship.

Therefore all human incarnate beings who live in a state of aware connection and flow WILL manifest the twin flame romantic relationship (if this is in alignment with their original blueprinted preincarnate map or destiny plan in accordance with their free will).

The majority of service-to-others incarnated starseeds WILL have this choice within their blueprint due to the high level of expansion that is afforded the soul when they move into the twin flame mirrored match as a romantic relationship.

Even those individuals who made the choice NOT to experience the twin flame mirrored match can choose to change this choice and 'remake the map' if you will, and that mirrored match, for them, when in flow, WILL be presented for them. Therefore from this perspective, every incarnated physical being has a twin flame in the form of a potential partner within a romantic relationship.

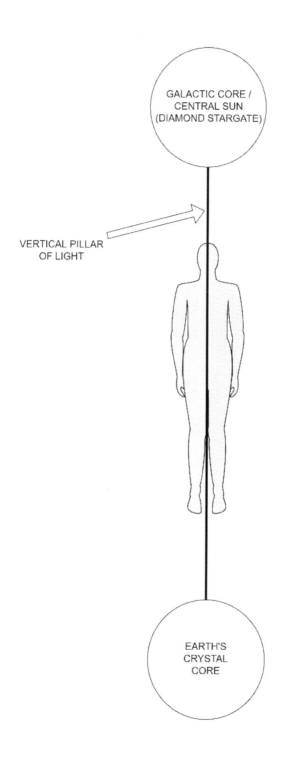

GALACTIC CORE /
CENTRAL SUN
(DIAMOND STARGATE)

VERTICAL PILLAR
OF LIGHT

EARTH'S
CRYSTAL
CORE

Above: The vertical axis (pillar of light)

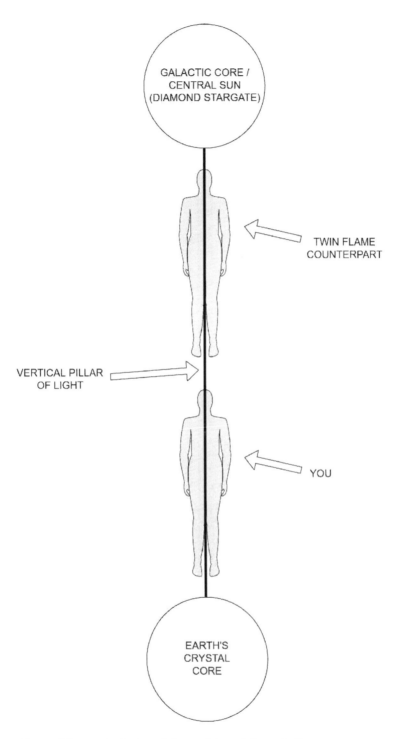

Above: A linear depiction of the position of the twin flame counterpart

We have spoken much of the vertical axis or the vertical pillar of light and if processing has not yet occurred for you as to why the vertical pillar of light is so significant within the twin flame manifestation, then know that the keys, codes and triggers have been presented for you within this transmission thus far.

We repeat, the keys, codes and triggers have been presented for you within this transmission thus far.

How are these triggers and codes presented through the written word? Indeed, we shall come to this point!

If, within your physical incarnation, you are an individual who lives within flow with the 'upward moving stream' and the 'downward moving stream' intertwining like a coiled spiral around the vertical pillar of light then you WILL process this information. This may occur within dreamtime, meditation or quiet contemplation. Often the connection to water will allow that electromagnetic flow to 'power up' if you will. Therefore if you immerse your physical body within water, especially if this mirrors your oceans with the salts provided (we speak here of Celtic sea salt baths or Epsom salt baths), then this allows the flow specific to the triggers to that which links your intention to the processing of the concept. Many a 'clairvoyant/precognitive vision' comes to those conduits of flow when immersed within the water.

The right hemisphere of the brain contains all the knowledge as a 'language' and is processed through the left hemisphere of the brain. Therefore if you have not yet moved into processing of the concept of the vertical axis of the matrix and its relation to the twin flame consciousness, we provide a different set of keys, codes and triggers for you that can be directly received and evaluated via the metaphor and symbolism found in both art and story.

Regarding art, we would draw your attention to the artistic depiction of that which you know as 'the caduceus'.

The Caduceus

The caduceus depicts the vertical axis of the matrix and the two intertwining streams that move along the axis. This is also a depiction of your 'awakened cellular memory' or 'activated DNA', also symbolising that which you know as the 'kundalini rising'.

Whilst you may not be aware within full interpretation or analysis of the codes and keys within the caduceus, all individuals who stand within flow will feel the calling of this symbol.

The symbol of the caduceus is a language in itself, so allow it to speak to you. Just spending time looking at the caduceus artwork will trigger those keys and codes you are looking for.

To bypass full processing is often the most aligned way to fully make use of these codes of information. For when one stands in flow, one stands within knowing... yet the knowing is within the DNA, within the heart. These are the important doorways or 'stargates' within self. The DNA and the heart. Full intellectual understanding within left brained understanding is not needed for the construction of the matrix and the embracing of the twin flame consciousness. Yet if you desire this (and anyone holding the indigo frequency will desire this), then the caduceus symbol will give you the keys and codes needed for processing.

The Story

The storyteller is the dreamweaver. The storyteller weaves the dream for the dreamwalkers (those who receive the dream and interact consciously with the dream). The dreamweavers are those who receive the codes and, in full flow, allow manifestation of the higher reality and thus the twin flame consciousness within their lives.

Our conduit Magenta Pixie in her merge with us, the White Winged Collective Consciousness of Nine, stands as the dreamweaver. As she formulates the story, or weaves the dream, we are the aspects of the right hemisphere of the brain that presents as she bypasses the left brained understanding. Therefore 'we' as the Nine are the DNA and the heart of our conduit (as that which is the cosmic 'WE' is the DNA and the heart of all things), therefore Magenta Pixie presents the story and we present the keys and codes needed within. These are bypassed by Magenta Pixie so even she herself will not be processing the meaning of the metaphors and symbols used within the story. This is the utilising of the cosmic language, that which you know as 'the language of light'.

The language of light is to be utilised by all who stand in flow and all who are moving into flow. Therefore each of you who read these words know and speak this language. For you would not have found your way to these words if you were not standing in flow or moving into flow. The synchronicity that occurs in your life as you walk your human path of physicality is the manifested mirrored match to the coordinates and codes that you have fed into your matrix. Therefore, embrace the mirrored match to your own matrix presentation as we give you the story...

The story presents with the perspective 'everyone has a twin flame'. When we look at this perspective, we see the vertical pillar of light, the 'as above, so below' linear presentation of physical self/higher self, with higher self at the upper point of the vertical pillar standing as the twin flame.

The vertical pillar of light, as part of the sixth dimensional star tetrahedron matrix construct, begins to create form from the geometries through vibration as light and sound. Therefore the mirrored match to the twin flame higher self construct is created within the physically incarnated individual's life.

When that individual stands within flow, holding the healthy activated matrix, then the mirrored match of the twin flame consciousness presented as a romantic relationship holding twin flame potential must and will manifest.

For those who do not stand in flow or hold the healthy activated matrix, the first step is to release that which you know as 'blocks' or 'traumas' and allow flow into the matrix and into self through what many may call 'shadow work', emotional integration and the understanding of the belief systems and paradigms as a feed system into the matrix field. This material is covered in our previous transmission, *Masters of the Matrix.*

Shadow Work

Therefore when the blocks/traumas are removed or unravelled and flow is created or resumed, the twin flame frequency must and will flow into the physically incarnated being and manifest as the mirrored match.

This is the case with all consciousness structures. Within the consciousness structures incarnated as 'humans on Earth' then this manifests as a romantic relationship (unless the individual is sovereign, working with 'high magick' and has created the desire to not experience the twin flame relationship). This manifests as a romantic relationship as it is through the 'relationship with other' that the human individual learns, develops, grows and expands and none is so close as the romantic or sexual relationship.

When flow is in place between both individuals, the masculine and feminine 'divine marriage' or 'inner alchemical merge' takes place. This occurs in the case of either the heterosexual or the homosexual relationship as gender is not the aspect that creates the mirrored match. The energetic system creates the mirrored match, therefore gender or sexual persuasion matters not when it comes to the manifestation of the twin flame energetic as a romantic and/or sexual relationship.

The Divine Triangle

When the merge between masculine and feminine takes place within the twin flame couple, that twin flame couple become an individualised consciousness in itself creating the formation of the divine triangle.

The first aspect of the divine triangle with the point upwards, represents the twin flame relationship itself and the second point of the triangle, locking together with the first triangle but pointing downwards to form the diamond, is the creative aspect and thus the creation itself birthed from the twin flame couple.

We therefore have two geometries here. The first triangle, which includes three aspects as the male, the female and the male/female merge (again we speak here of energies and these energies may or may not be reflected within gender). Then we have the second or downward pointing triangle, which includes three aspects as the male, the female and the child (we speak here of energies and the child may or may not be an actual, physical, literal child).

We look at the true unified pyramid or diamond and this we can present to you: that the diamond light or the diamond matrix is the same energetic as the twin flame. The diamond light and the twin flame are one and the same energy.

These entire geometries can be expressed and indeed will be expressed within one person.

Therefore one incarnated person can express the male, the female, the male/female merge and the child as the true unified pyramid (or interlocking triads) or diamond light matrix and thus the twin flame energetic. When one individual meets another individual and both individuals hold the individualised divine marriage, alchemical merge, diamond light matrix and twin flame energetic, then the twin flame potential is automatically expressed within that couple (even if they are not presenting as a romantic relationship). They may hold a potential romantic relationship that is not set to actualise within that incarnation or they may be parent/child, sibling, friend or business partner connections that hold a twin flame potential.

These are patterns of actualised geometry and they manifest in a myriad of different ways. The actualised geometry we speak of is a living intelligence, a consciousness in its own right, a 'divine architecture' if you will, and like all consciousness structures it can be communicated with. It may present in many forms.

Matrix Mastery

Learning to navigate this geometric grid or divine architecture within your life is what we would call 'Matrix Mastery' or 'high magick', also known to many as enlightenment or self-actualisation.

Within the perspective of 'everyone has a twin flame', we can move into more of a literal and linear sense and embrace this perspective as an actual physical romantic and/or sexual relationship with a partner.

We are looking here at the 'high magickal work' of manifesting a twin flame relationship into your life and the recognition of that relationship when it does show up in your life. The first step is the embracing of flow, in order to free fall the higher energetics into third dimensional manifestation.

If a relationship (even one with twin flame potential) is embraced within an individual (or couple) where there is not a full state of flow, then the energetic matches to the blocks (traumas and shadow realities) will also be manifested as the mirrored match within the relationship. Therefore one will hold the intensity of the twin flame union and still be holding a flawed, incohesive geometry within that relationship. Hence why many teachers of the twin flame relationship will tell you that a 'twin flame relationship will not come into your life until you are ready for it'.

This is true only from the perspective of the full flow creating a full mirrored match and creativity within the divine feminine/sacred masculine merge. One indeed can manifest a twin flame potential relationship even when one is not 'ready' for that relationship.

Indeed it is the 'flawed relationship' if you will (holding the mirrored match to blocks, shadow realities and traumas) that assists in the readiness of that relationship as the relationship itself is a trigger to expansion, growth and awareness.

The relationship that embodies the twin flame frequency is always a relationship of 'higher service' if you will, that which serves the whole and it does this by serving the self (and the relationship as an individualised entity) with its expansion. If self is served expansion, this then filters into the macrocosmic aspect of self and the greater reality at large.

Flow and Shadow Work

Let us suppose then that we have two women, to use as examples. We have Lucy and we have Katie.

Lucy stands within a state of flow as she has worked on herself for a long time, is aware of the chakra system, the energetic system and the matrix reality and her place within it. She is aware of sovereignty and the path towards sovereignty.

Katie is very similar. She too stands mostly in flow and she too holds conscious awareness of the chakra system and the energetic system.

Lucy has worked on her 'shadow side' if you will. She has unravelled past experiences and traumas, even moving beyond her current incarnation to do this work.

Katie on the other hand, holds shadow traumas that she is unaware of. They have not made themselves known to her consciously at this point in her life. There will therefore be a part of Katie's energetic stream that does not filter through in a state of flow. This aspect is 'small' if you will, within Katie's entire energetic system therefore Katie is still able to create the mirrored match into her reality of the twin flame relationship.

Lucy and Katie both connect with twin flame partners. This is an example and there are many permeations of outcomes with actual individuals as we are looking at such a complicated matrix with many pathways. The examples presented here are indeed most simplified.

The Vesica Piscis

Yet the most probable outcome with these two ladies is that Lucy will manifest a twin flame relationship match (if we base this purely on her level of light quotient and level of flow).

This twin flame relationship is most likely to stand within the geometric formation of the vesica piscis geometry (the divine feminine and the sacred masculine and the creativity that is birthed from that union).

Lucy is most likely to create a sustainable relationship holding the twin flame geometry and bringing the twin flame experience.

With Katie, the situation is more complex. With each individiual there are many timelines dependent on thoughts, words, actions, deeds, visualisations and emotions within that individual. Let us for example suggest that Katie has two probable pathways in front of her... timeline 1 and timeline 2.

Within timeline 1, Katie continues to work on her traumas and her 'shadow side' if you will. What is therefore most likely to manifest for her is a twin flame relationship that holds the probability of the vesica piscis as a potential rather than a manifested actuality. Katie in timeline 1 may not realise this person holds the twin flame energetic for her so she will be asking herself questions and making statements like "Is this person my twin flame?" or "I don't think this person is my twin flame."

She may be looking at other potential partners or actively trying to manifest other partners into her life believing she is NOT with her twin flame match.

We may say to you now that Katie in the timeline 1 situation is very, very common amongst you. What happens here could branch off into two other potentials. Potential A and potential B.

In potential A, Katie stays with the partner, continues to work on herself and eventually the twin flame potential becomes an actuality within her relationship. Creativity stands between the divine feminine and sacred masculine fields and Katie finally realises she was with 'her twin flame' the entire time.

In potential B, Katie decides to leave the relationship. She continues working on herself and manifests a new partner into her life who stands as the mirrored match to the twin flame frequency. Creativity is instant between the couple and the divine feminine and sacred masculine merge stands in balance. Katie within timeline 1 potential B will be able to say, "I was not with my twin flame so I did the right thing to leave that relationship and now I have found my twin flame."

Both Katie timeline 1 potential A and potential B are correct in their statements. Either potential is a win-win situation for Katie in timeline 1 because she has worked upon her traumas and her shadow realities and lives within a state of continued expansion and growth.

Katie timeline 2 does NOT work on the shadow aspects and the traumas. They remain buried even though they are a small part of the overall aspect of Katie. Katie's relationship will therefore reflect the partially awakened and expanded aspect of herself, and the part aspect that stands in shadow and is buried.

With Katie timeline 2 we can also project two potential pathways. Potential A and potential B.

Katie timeline 2 potential A is a reality where the *relationship itself* acts as a trigger to the buried shadow aspect. The relationship holds challenges directly relating to the shadow aspect and throws light on the shadow aspect again and again until finally Katie is forced to look at the shadow aspect and unravel the energy of it. The twin flame relationship then springs into its fullest manifestation and Katie timeline 2 potential A is able to say, "This twin flame relationship is the best thing that has ever happened to me as it has assisted me in unravelling this trauma and moving forward."

Katie timeline 2 potential A is then able to merge with Katie timeline 1 (either potential) and also stands within the win-win situation.

Katie timeline 2 potential B also has a relationship constantly throwing light upon the shadow aspect but in potential B, Katie refuses to look at the trauma. Instead she rebounds the blame onto the relationship itself and all the energetics within the shadow trauma become superimposed upon her relationship. Katie can then either stay in a dysfunctional relationship or leave the relationship altogether. Either way, Katie will come to the conclusion that, "I am not in a twin flame relationship and my partner is not my twin flame."

Katie will feel disillusioned and hard done by. The external influence of the buried shadow trauma will continue to spring up for Katie in all walks of life but most especially within the relationship (or lack of it). The twin flame potential cannot possibly actualise due to the shadow trauma that remains buried. Katie timeline 2 potential B is a situation that is also very common on your planet.

The first three Katies in the win-win situation will manifest their twin flame. The fourth Katie will not enter a win-win situation and will not manifest her twin flame (even when in both timeline 1 and timeline 2 the twin flame partner is the same person!).

We draw your attention here to the perspective that the twin flame relationship AND the twin flame partner are direct manifestations of your own consciousness.

The Influence of Belief Systems and Emotions

We could look here at more examples of how your own belief systems and emotions influence (or indeed create) your reality. Using examples specific to the twin flame manifested relationship.

Let us take two young men, George and John.

George and John would both like to be in relationships that hold the twin flame energetic.

George and John have both worked upon themselves. George has done extensive work on himself including integration of emotions. We would direct you to the aspect within our previous transmission *Masters of the Matrix* to a chapter entitled 'Emotional Integration' for information on this integrative work.

John has also done energy work, chakra clearing and shadow/trauma work on himself.

The difference between George and John is that George stands in a state of peace with his current 'single' status, whilst he would like to be in a relationship (most especially a relationship that fits the twin flame energetic).

George, whilst he would love a relationship, is happy to be single. He is joyful and loving in himself, towards himself and sees a very positive future for himself either single or as part of a couple. George therefore manifests a win-win situation for himself (all timelines and realities he experiences within the quantum field are a direct match to his emotional equilibrium, positive outlook and self love). It therefore does not matter to George if he manifests a twin flame relationship into his reality or not, for he already embraces the twin flame consciousness and the 'divine marriage' within himself.

George will manifest the twin flame relationship into his life as the geometries within the sixth dimensional matrix of self will naturally create the codes needed for the mirrored match in matter and form. George is happy and fulfilled as a single man and is happy and fulfilled within the twin flame relationship which holds the geometry of the vesica piscis and is sustainable. The twin flame relationship holds longevity and assists both individuals to move further into growth, expansion and enlightenment.

John on the other hand, is NOT happy to be single. He desperately wants to be in a relationship and specifically a twin flame relationship. He has worked upon himself, moved through shadow work including past life regression work. He has many friends around him but a relationship has not come into his life.

He feels he has a lot to offer a relationship and is quite upset that he has not manifested this into his life. He feels lonely and sad, to the point of being mildly depressed about this situation. The longer his single status goes on, the more he becomes angry that this relationship has not occurred for him.

Whilst all John's emotions are perfectly understandable and natural given his situation, he is creating the mirrored match for himself of 'not having a relationship' despite the work he has done on himself in other areas of his life (although there would still be some buried trauma in order for John to feel unhappy about being single in the first place).

What John is doing here, is feeding codes into his matrix of loneliness, sadness, despair and anger regarding being single. The sixth dimensional matrix is therefore creating the mirrored match to these emotional codes within John's reality and he remains single. He continues to be in a situation where he does not attract a relationship.

The Codes of Integration

For John to be able to move forward with his goal of a twin flame relationship, John needs to create the twin flame consciousness as an energy throughout his being. Then the matrix codes will create the mirrored match in form and matter.

John's first step is the emotional integration process.

Once the emotions move into the processing stage, the matrix 'phires up' if you will, it begins to spin, weaving a web of light around itself. It 'clears' and it 'upgrades' and the codes of 'integration' are the codes that manifest within form and matter.

Integration itself is a very high vibratory state, and this in itself shifts timelines allowing flow and allowing the twin flame match to come into John's life.

The twin flame relationship may present itself as a possibility at this point as it is part of an integrated life for John as he lines up with his desires.

As John processes the emotion and integrates that emotion, he will be able to let go of the resistance to 'not having a relationship'. He will move into acceptance of being single and begin to allow the flow of the twin flame consciousness into his being. It is at this point that the presented potential of the twin flame relationship becomes manifested actuality and John moves into that relationship.

Hence the reason why many spiritual teachings on your planet will say 'let go' or 'surrender'.

These concepts can appear meaningless if they are not concepts that you have consciously processed or experienced. The emotional integration *is* the letting go and *it is* the surrender, but this does not mean 'release' a negative emotion by simply not feeling it.

Many teachings speak of releasing or transcending emotion, and there are many who instantly process the meaning of this release or transcendence.

Other individuals simply feel inadequate or that they have somehow failed spiritually because they continue to feel negative emotion.

Yet the negative emotion itself is a 'message' if you will, and it is a 'signpost' that shows you where you are. The feeling of the negative emotion is the first step into emotional integration. The understanding of this process will assist you in transforming negative emotional codes into codes of integration into your matrix. This allows integration to be the mirrored match within your reality. The form of an 'integrated life' assists in moving from chaos into clarity, which allows higher flow. The higher flow is a direct merge between your higher self and your physical self. The higher self, as we have said, *is* the true twin flame. When higher flow is received and integrated, then the mirrored match of 'twin flame consciousness' is actualised within a manifested state within your reality. One of the most aligned methods for the manifestation of the twin flame consciousness is a twin flame relationship (or one that holds twin flame potential).

Therefore everyone has a twin flame. This is the explanation of that perspective.

The Second Perspective - No One Has a Twin Flame

This perspective is much easier to explain. We would first mention a few words about 'perspective' itself. There is a perspective for every belief system and construct within that belief system. There are extremes at either side of a spectrum of belief systems, if you will, and a myriad of perspectives in-between this.

Within a third dimensional reality, belief systems will be finite and have boundaries. Sometimes healthy boundaries, and sometimes these will equate to restrictions depending on the individual. When an individual moves into an expansive way of thinking, they open up their perception to embrace more and more perspectives (that perhaps would have been incongruent and opposing before the expansive state).

The expansive thinkers move into a situation where they embrace more and more perspectives themselves, yet they also begin to understand and empathise with belief systems that they themselves would not, could not and do not embrace (for example, a service-to-others polarised individual embracing a service-to-self perspective).

Their empathy does not mean that they resonate or agree with the perspective, but that they are able to understand it. The way an individual moves through higher dimensions of consciousness is through the embracing of these different perspectives.

We repeat - *The way an individual moves through higher dimensions of consciousness is through the embracing of these different perspectives.*

We show you now the perspective of 'no one has a twin flame'.

Just because this perspective exists does not mean that you need to embrace it if you choose not to do so. Embracing this perspective simply gives you a 'bigger playing field' within which to operate.

Embracing this perspective within your belief system does not negate the opposing presented perspective of 'everyone has a twin flame' as long as you embrace that perspective simultaneously to the other one. This takes you into an expansive and multidimensional awareness relative to the twin flame philosophies and consciousness specifically.

The perspective of 'no one has a twin flame' would come from the premise that there is no such thing as a 'twin flame'. The perspective here would be looking at a 'twin flame counterpart' as being one individual.

There is a perspective where this is not an aligned belief system (as the twin flame manifests through many and indeed all individuals), although indeed other perspectives are incongruent to this one (we shall come to these).

The other angle to the perspective of 'no one has a twin flame', as in 'there is no such thing as a twin flame', would stem from either... a) There is no such thing as a 'higher self', therefore there cannot be a 'twin flame', or b) The twin flame *is* the higher self and therefore not a person (as in an incarnated individual).

These are indeed more limited perspectives than the previous perspective of 'everyone has a twin flame' and we could place these in a third dimensional (or within some individuals a fourth dimensional) way of thinking.

Each dimension holds a different set of perspectives. Indeed one could say there are different truths relative to each dimensional field. No less more truthful than the other, simply less expansive.

So we would present to you that 'no one has a twin flame' as predominantly a third dimensional perspective when looking at the point of view that the twin flame counterpart is *one person and one person alone.*

We have to place this perspective 'no one has a twin flame' within the third dimensional thought process as it does not account for destiny. Destiny will always present *one twin flame, and one twin flame alone* (but that is a different perspective).

So, 'no one has a twin flame' is based on the premise that a *twin flame is only one person* and that you as humans, incarnate on Earth, may experience many loving, romantic and/or sexual relationships within your lifetime and that it is unhelpful to view the twin flame as only one potential partner.

Indeed the embracing of the 'there is only one twin flame' perspective does limit the universal flow surrounding the individual with that belief system, cutting off the higher dimensional matrix flow into the creation of the twin flame consciousness within form and matter.

Therefore embracing the perspective of 'no one has a twin flame' simultaneously to 'there is only one twin flame' would open up the expansive belief system and feed those simultaneous coordinates and codes into the matrix. This would make the actualisation of the twin flame relationship within the third dimensional experience far more likely due to the opening up of flow.

To embrace the perspective 'no one has a twin flame' may cut you off from experiencing an actual twin flame relationship... yet equally, it may not.

If your belief system holds that of 'well suited partners moving into constructive and positive relationships' then you may well experience the twin flame relationship without subscribing to the belief system of it.

Perspective Itself is the Teaching

An interesting pairing between twin flame couples that is most common at this point upon your planet is the partner who strongly believes in 'twin flames' and the other that does not believe in twin flames at all.

We see a disharmonious energetic between these matching partners created by these belief systems, yet in actuality both partners embrace correct perspectives.

This is the case for a great many subjects and concepts, not just the concept of the twin flame. Therefore 'perspective itself' is the teaching delivered here through this aspect of this transmission.

If you can embrace the perspective of another, even just through understanding and empathy without actually subscribing fully to it, or opening one's awareness into the *possibility* of that perspective, then harmonious energetic flow can be restored.

A third dimensional explanation for this would present as 'making a compromise', however this is not so easy for an incarnated physical individual who thinks multidimensionally.

Let us show you an example.

In this example, we have a couple... Louise and Stephen.

Louise remembers a time when Stephen told her he wanted to write a novel about vampires. Louise reminds Stephen of this. Stephen has no recollection of ever suggesting he wanted to write a novel about vampires.

Stephen suggests Louise's memory is wrong, or that it is her agenda that she is manipulating Stephen into as she *wants* him to write a novel about vampires. Louise suggests Stephen is very forgetful or is deliberately hiding the fact that he wanted to write a novel about vampires.

Disharmonious energetic flow ensues between the couple that can take hold as mistrust and suspicion. Unity between the couple is impaired and integration becomes disintegration. This plants a potential seed for the end of the relationship. Not because Stephen has not written a vampire fiction novel but because each individual believes their own memory system, concluding that the other person is incorrect.

The Mandela Effect

If Stephen were to embrace the possibility that he *did* once say he wanted to write a vampire novel, and if Louise were to embrace the possibility that she imagined the whole thing, this may go some way to reinstating harmonious flow and thus trust and integration. However, this may also lead to incongruity within the individual's thinking and as expansive, service-to-others individuals they stand strong within their own awareness and hold a strong sense of memory pathway activity and paradigm. This is most likely if they are 'twin flames' in the first place.

Therefore Stephen suggests another explanation for this difference in memory. What if Louise and Stephen hold memories from different timelines? What if Stephen *did* say he wanted to write a vampire novel in the timeline Louise remembers? *Yet he did not ever* say this in the timeline which he remembers?

They would both be correct but one may perceive that they hold high imaginative or distorted thinking. Yet if they were to embrace this as a *possibility* then not only would they restore harmonious flow, trust and integration within their twin flame relationship, but they would also be embracing a truthful, aligned aspect of reality. That of 'timeline convergence' or 'overlap' or 'jumping' known to many of you as 'the Mandela effect'.

It may be that one of the individuals is simply forgetful, yet it may also indeed be that they are remembering actions that occurred in different timelines.

Time wraps itself inside out and upside down and around itself, twisting and merging in the process. It is not a linear process and you 'hop' from timeline to timeline regularly.

Therefore the twin flame relationship in itself has created an expansive way of thinking for the concept of time and timelines, just through the desire to connect with one's partner in a harmonious way and 'come to a compromise'.

This occurs with twin flame couples all the time for they are within what we would call a 'contracted relationship', indeed a 'destiny' if you will.

To recap for this perspective...

'No one has a twin flame' stems from the belief system that a *twin flame is only one person.* From this perspective, this is a correct premise for universal flow and thus 'twin flame' flow can manifest through anyone. Therefore no one has a twin flame.

'No one has a twin flame' can also come from the premise that the twin flame is the same thing as the 'higher self' and that there is no such thing as a higher self therefore there is *no such thing as a twin flame.*

This is also a correct premise if you take the non-linear viewpoint as the self being everything and all there is as one. Therefore there is nothing outside of self, there is only self.

When looking at the vertical axis of the matrix, the vertical pillar of light within the non-linear viewpoint, there is only self standing within that vertical axis. An aligned and correct perspective.

'No one has a twin flame' can also come from the premise that the twin flame *is* the higher self. Therefore within this perspective, one subscribes to the viewpoint that the higher self exists. The higher self and the twin flame are one. The twin flame resides in a higher dimension *not* in the physical dimension, therefore the twin flame is *not a person*. This premise still implies a belief in the twin flame energy (as the higher self) but *not* in the twin flame as an incarnated individual. Therefore it would still fit the perspective of 'no one has a twin flame'.

This is a correct premise. If you look at the vertical axis, the vertical pillar of light in the vertical linear sense, you see the superimposed higher energy body 'above' the physical body. This is the higher self or indeed 'twin flame' aspect (and this may manifest to you as an actual twin flame or twin soul partner assisting you from the higher dimensions - also very common within your starseed communities). This twin flame aspect is an individualised consciousness and cannot be replicated upon the physical level (from the linear perspective only), therefore 'no one has a twin flame' is a correct perspective.

This explains that perspective.

The Third Perspective - Everyone is One's Twin Flame

This perspective is somewhat similar to the first perspective, 'everyone has a twin flame', but not quite. This perspective is suggesting that *everyone* is your twin flame. *Everyone? Everyone on planet Earth? And beyond?* Is this a correct perspective? The answer to that is, yes.

This perspective of 'everyone is one's twin flame' is based on the premise of unity and oneness.

If you or indeed 'we' are all one, we are all one being that includes the 'we' as us (the White Winged Collective Consciousness of Nine), then we are each ourselves. We are you and vice versa. If you look at the reflected reality to this as manifesting within the third dimension, this suggests every single person you meet is a potential twin flame for they are you. If the higher self aspect is your twin flame and your higher self aspect is the same aspect as everyone else's higher self (as in Source), then everyone is you and therefore your twin flame and you manifest this unified thinking within the third dimension. This is reflected in your third dimension due to the codes and coordinates fed into your matrix system which create the mirrored match in form and matter.

This perspective allows for polygamy and open relationships, as well as one-on-one 'twin flame' relationships.

If one embraces this perspective, one sees that those who share a 'twin flame' relationship with several partners at the same time, or with several different partners individually over the course of many years, are embracing aligned flow and higher geometric pattern. These individuals, whilst different to 'the norm', embrace higher dimensional thinking, higher spirituality, high magick, ascension and enlightenment.

The down side to this perspective may be that the individual does not embrace that unique merge with one other person that comes with the 'partner of destiny', as the codes may or may not have been fed into the matrix to create that pattern.

However this does not mean an individual does not embrace 'twin flame frequency' or cannot have a 'twin flame relationship' (or relationships).

This is a most aligned perspective to embrace if you are stuck in the thinking that 'there is only one twin flame for me on the whole planet' (especially if you have decided who that person is and that person does not share your perspective! ... again, most common within your third dimensional experience).

To embrace this perspective fully and to commit to it allows surrender from the resistance you will have created by holding the belief system that there is only one twin flame for you. When the resistance to that belief is released, this feeds a twin flame knowing into your matrix system and gives that 'larger playing field' if you will, within the universal 'form and matter' match to your matrix presentation.

The perspective 'everyone is one's twin flame' is based on the premise that we are all one soul, all one being and that the twin flame energy can be reflected through everybody... making everyone, everywhere, your twin flame.

This explains that perspective.

Yet More Perspectives

There are yet more perspectives naturally, for every perspective you could conceive of is a perspective that holds merit, if the original belief system, the premise, holds congruency with the perspective itself.

Perspectives are created by the belief system in order to open into expansion and higher thinking and also in order to remain within a constricted, narrow belief system so that shadow aspects do not have to be bought to the fore and looked at.

Perspectives validate negative and positive belief systems and the same perspective may validate a negative belief in one individual and a positive belief in another.

There is one perspective we would draw your attention to now that is the most common perspective within third and fourth dimensional thinking. Even within fifth dimensional thinkers, this perspective is held. We have touched upon this perspective somewhat within our explanations of the first three perspectives. This perspective is that of 'there is only one twin flame'.

Are we saying that this perspective is incorrect? No. This is also a correct perspective, yet this belief system can be either very positive and expansive or very negative and restrictive. Here's why...

If an individual holds the belief that there is only one twin flame for them, they could be coming from a place of 'knowing their destiny' which, depending on how the belief system is arranged, can trigger expansion or restriction.

Let us take two examples of individuals who hold this belief system. One within expansion (Mary), and one within restriction (Diana).

This, again, is a simplified explanation and in truth an incarnated individual's matrix field is far more complex with infinite potential timelines and probable paths available for them within any belief system, especially within such a deep and expansive topic as twin flames.

We look now at these simplified examples of Mary and Diana.

Free Will and Destiny Walk Hand in Hand

Mary holds an expansive belief system relative to the concept 'there is only one twin flame'. In order to hold this belief system within expansion, Mary will have journeyed through a multiperspective belief system and will have become aware of the other perspectives regarding the twin flame consciousness. Mary will be aware of the concept that 'free will and destiny walk hand in hand'.

Mary will be aware of the preincarnate blueprint and the fact that her entire life is mapped out for her before she is even born. She will therefore understand what 'destiny' means. She will understand what a 'partner of destiny' is and she will also understand that she creates her own reality.

She will be walking in complete alignment with her blueprint, walking within a constant convergence point or 'node point' within her blueprint. Her belief system, emotional responses to her belief system and actions based on those emotional responses will create the blueprint that shows *the same twin flame partner in every timeline.* Therefore, regarding Mary's twin flame partner, she *has no free will.* The reason why she has no free will is because she walks in perfect alignment with that which is predetermined. Her desires, wants, belief systems and knowings are all in exact alignment to the predetermined blueprint. She has chosen this path through her expansion. She has chosen this path through her free will. Therefore the path that gives her no free will is the path that simultaneously gives her the *greatest* free will. Mary lives a life embracing zero point energy and from that point there ceases to be any past or future. There is only the present, only the one moment. From that perspective, there ceases to be a blueprint! There is only creation.

Through Mary's understanding of her self as a master creator, she chooses to embrace destiny, knowing her guidance system of light always leads her, through synchronicity and high magick, to the path that is best for her on all levels. She projects this belief system into the twin flame consciousness that flows through her and within her.

Because she exists within this conscious awareness and state of expansion, there can be only 'destiny' for her. The preincarnate blueprint is the same pathway as her choices in her current 'now' moment. This belief system, awareness and expansion can lead only to destiny and within that destiny the twin flame consciousness, as a mirror to the higher energetic stream of the full individualised matrix system (not just the vertical pillar of light but the entire dodecahedron presentation), will manifest the 'partner of destiny' as the one true twin flame.

From the zero point field, preincarnate destiny paradigm, there can be only one twin flame. The belief system that Mary holds is an expansive one therefore she will naturally attract the twin flame partner within a twin flame relationship of longevity. It is important to note the level of expansion Mary is at in order to achieve this reality for herself. She has *already* embraced the other twin flame perspectives within her integration process and her journey.

Could Mary move 'backwards' and 'demanifest' the partner of destiny/one true twin flame?

This is rare but possible. Rare once an individual achieves this level of expansion as they raise their light quotient with expansive states and thus the level of service-to-others polarisation. Once an individual has achieved this state it is most unlikely they would 'go backwards' if you will, and begin to demanifest that which they have manifested.

However this *can* happen. If an individual were to 'break the circle of love' if you will, for an extended period of time... then they would move out of the zero point field and lose expansion/light quotient and service-to-others polarisation.

What is the Circle of Love?

This is a metaphoric presentation of unity within an incarnated individual. It is the projected visual reality of an individual standing within a circle, holding unconditional love space for every being that surrounds her, completing the circle. Each being surrounding her within the circle are other incarnated individuals upon her planet... animals, plants, crystals, elementals, extraterrestrials and other non-temporal entities including fourth dimensional 'trapped' spirits. This would include all beings of a negative polarisation and the entire service-to-self structures and the individualised beings within those structures.

If *just one* entity is looked upon through negative emotion (fear, anger, hatred, jealousy and so on) *for an extended period of time* then this causes a break or rupture within that circle of love. This leads to loss of expansion/light quotient and service-to-others polarisation. An expansive individual will always stand within lovelight and lightlove. This manifests as 'unconditional love for all' through the heart centre even if, and especially when, healthy boundaries are exercised within the third dimensional reality. (Meaning one can feel love, forgiveness and acceptance within the actual emotional field for a person or consciousness structure, but chooses not to engage with, or keeps at a distance, or does not lend energy to that person or consciousness structure... within the third dimension).

How Long is an Extended Period of Time?

This would be impossible to accurately calculate as this is linear time combined with intensity of negative emotion (linear time being shorter when intensity of negative emotion is higher due to prolonged sustainability of profound negative emotion being extremely difficult for polarised service-to-others individuals or those moving towards that polarisation), but as a general rule we would be talking months rather than weeks or years on a linear level.

Time will always be given for the processing of negative emotion before this affects light quotient. The majority of starseeds or lightworkers on your planet are moving through negative emotions towards one single individual in a matter of hours, and are processing negative emotions towards group consciousness structures within days or sometimes weeks.

Even long-term negative emotion can be processed. For example... a son who has not spoken to his father in twenty years, and has held negative emotion towards him for that amount of time, can still process these emotions and begin or resume light quotient levels.

Again, we stress how very rare this situation is. The majority of individuals at zero point field levels will not move 'backwards' if you will, and lose light quotient. Especially so, given the current electromagnetic energetics upon your third density Earth due to the way this light 'holds' the higher frequencies in ways that has not occurred on your planet before.

We move now to the example of Diana.

Diana holds the belief system of 'there is only one twin flame' through a restrictive belief. She may subscribe to the simplified metaphor of the incarnational split, where each soul is half male and half female. The soul splits into two. One half incarnates as a female human being in third density, the other as a male in human density.

This is a metaphor for the duality that occurs as higher dimensional consciousness becomes manifest within physical matter. The duality will be a male/female consciousness that will be inherent in all things, not an actual male human and a female human. The twin flame frequency can exist within same sex pairings as much as within opposite sex pairings. The duality is experienced as 'contrast' within the third dimension for your growth and expansion. The male/female polarity is only one example of the duality experienced within the third dimension.

Yet for someone experiencing linear time and third dimensional thinking, describing the twin flame energy as a soul splitting in half, goes someway to explaining the very accurate models of polarity and duality that you experience.

Therefore subscribing to the belief of the twin souls splitting into two can understandably lead to a belief that there is only one twin flame.

The True Twin Split

A more accurate way to explain the 'splitting' of a soul (and all souls are whole and intact, a perfect copy of original Source... when they split they produce identical holographic copies of one another, not a half of one and a half of the other) would be to say one half of the soul remains within the higher dimensions as one half of that twin, and the other half moves into matter. Hence the perspective of the higher self being the one true twin flame.

The other perspective that may lead to a constrictive belief regarding having only one twin flame partner is the linear interpretation of destiny. As in 'there is only one destiny, therefore there is only one partner of destiny, therefore there is only one twin flame'.

Whilst in essence, when one looks at the quantum world and the way you experience this quantum world, then this premise is a correct one.

When this filters into a belief that there is only one, and there can be only one, and the individual *decides exactly who that one is*, then this leads to a constriction of energy.

This is the case with our example, Diana.

Diana has 'fallen in love' with another individual and has fully decided that this individual (let us name her Rachael) is her one true twin flame. Diana and Rachael have a relationship and Diana feels within her the knowings that she is bonded on a soul level with Rachael. Diana has 'memories' of past life incarnations with Rachael. All this, from Diana's perspective is correct and truthful.

But Rachael does not share this belief and decides to leave the relationship.

69

From Rachael's perspective, this is also correct for her. It may be that she is not bonded on a soul level to Diana (from her perspective) or the intensity of the relationship may be too much for her, or she may decide at this time that she does not want to be in a relationship. She may well be bonded on a soul level to Diana but does not remember this as she has not reached the awareness level that Diana holds. There may be many reasons why the relationship between Diana and Rachael is a vibrational mismatch. It may even be the case that Diana and Rachael *do* embody twin flame frequency but *'divine timing'* or synchronicity is at play here (as in their meeting is destined but a relationship of longevity is not). There are so many permeations to the experiences an individual may plan out for themselves before they incarnate into physical matter. These plans are created for the individual's highest good and highest expansion. Meeting, connecting with and moving away from the twin flame partner brings as much expansion to the soul as the relationship that holds longevity! (Depending on what it is that their soul needs to experience in that particular incarnation.)

Closed and Open Belief Systems

So in the case of Diana, who has been in a relationship with Rachael and has decided that Rachael is her one and only true twin flame for this lifetime, what is it that makes this belief a restrictive one?

It is the fact that the universe (an abundant flow of energy constantly presenting to you that which YOU create through the coordinates and codes you place into your matrix field) cannot present to Diana another partner matching the twin flame frequency. This is because Diana does not recognise that to be a reality. Therefore for Diana the 'promise of true love' for her can never be a probability or even a possibility for to her, *there is only one twin flame and that is Rachael.* Her belief system, holding the emotional feelings of loss, grief, rejection and even acceptance still create codes that match a reality where she has lost her one and only true love.

Even if Diana were to meet another partner and have another romantic relationship, that relationship could not match the twin flame frequency for that is outside the belief system that Diana holds.

When a belief system is that steadfast, the individual creates a reality to match their belief system (or that fits within their belief system) rather than the new reality itself being the trigger to change the belief system.

Only one slight change within the individual's belief system is needed in order to allow outside triggers to change belief systems, and that is holding an 'open belief system' rather than a closed one.

If Diana were to hold an open belief system then her belief of 'there is only one twin flame' would hold the potential of manifesting that actual belief as the belief *would no longer be constrictive.* An open belief system is an *expansive* one. A closed belief system is a *constrictive* one.

Examples of open and closed belief systems relative to Diana's twin flame belief would be:

1) There is only one twin flame and that is Rachael. (This is a closed belief system.)

2) There is only one twin flame and I believe this is probably Rachael. (This is an open belief system as it leaves room for change.)

3) There is only one twin flame and that is Rachael. However I am willing to accept that maybe my twin flame is someone else other than Rachael, or that maybe you can experience more than one twin flame in one lifetime. (This is an open belief system as it leaves room for change.)

To shift from a closed into an open belief system sometimes only needs the most minor adjustment in the individual's way of thinking.

We say to you now that *the only way to discover the truth of your reality is to open your belief systems. To hold a closed belief system leaves no room for change, yet change is the very fabric which reality is built upon. For change is movement, and consciousness is fluidity and movement. When you match your thinking to the fabric of reality, it will become fluid. There will always be room for change.*

The twin flame belief system is no different. Whilst there is indeed a true perspective of 'there is only one true twin flame'.

This perspective must be embraced with fluidity as an open belief system in order for the one true twin flame to manifest in your reality. Therefore a closed belief *cannot* manifest. Only an open belief system can actually manifest for you within your reality.

The Belief System Paradox

There are many ways in which one can open a belief system. One of the easiest ways to do this is to embrace the possibility of *the opposing belief.*

For example...

I believe in God *but I am prepared to accept that there is no God.* (Only by opening to the opposing belief can you hope to find God.)

Yet also we say to you, and we say to you most often... *stand strong in your knowing.*

How therefore can you stand strong in your knowing and yet still embrace the opposing perspective?

Using the above example, how does one stand strong in the knowing that there is a God (or Source, Prime Creator, infinite intelligence) yet maintain an open belief system that there might possibly be no God?

Standing strong within your knowing means simultaneously standing strong in your unknowing. For when you do this *you mirror the energy of Source.*

Let us make two statements that are both in absolute alignment with truth...

1) Source is all-knowing.

2) Source is constantly seeking to know itself.

When you do the same - stand strong in your knowing yet simultaneously open your belief system to the possibility that the *opposite* to your knowing may be correct - you move out of duality and polarity and into unity and oneness.

For you shall discover that there are many perspectives and when you can embrace two seemingly *opposing* perspectives, then you have found the key to expansion.

Let us look at our previous example...

I believe in God *but I am prepared to accept that there is no God.*

The opposing belief of 'there is no God'... could there be such a perspective whereby this could be true? These are the questions to ask yourself as you take your journey of expansion.

The answer to this question is, yes.

If we look at the second statement, 'Source is constantly seeking to know itself', then this would suggest that Source does not know itself. From that perspective this is the case. This is why *you* are here. To assist Source in discovering who and what it is.

It is true that Source is an all-knowing entity. Pure consciousness. Therefore Source exists. Therefore 'God' exists.

Yet it is also true that Source is NOT an all-knowing entity (for it seeks to know itself, it does this through *you* and *your* experiences as you exist within matter), therefore as it does not know itself it cannot know if it exists. Therefore it cannot know if 'God' exists.

There is the perspective you are looking for.

This expansive way of thinking can be applied to all things, all structures and all belief systems within your reality. We bring this transmission through our conduit at this time in order to assist you with this expansive way of thinking.

We say to you that the only way to find true knowing is to embrace the *unknowing.*

As you 'make known the unknown' (as is your higher mission within third dimensional Earth), you become aware of the unknown also.

It is said *the more you learn, the more you realise how little you know.* Indeed this is true for when you think this way, you mirror Source. All-knowing. Knowing all. For *Source is 'All'.* Yet what is 'All'? Source seeks to answer this question by experiencing *all and everything.* This includes *all perspectives.*

You, in matter, mirror this same expansion.

Therefore, let us move back to Diana's constrictive perspective of 'there is only one twin flame and that is Rachael'.

Diana has created a wall for herself. Anything beyond that wall (as in another person becoming her twin flame) cannot exist for her. Because she has created the wall for herself, within her belief system, the twin flame relationship *cannot manifest.* This is the reason why her relationship with Rachael did not work, for Diana cannot manifest a twin flame relationship of longevity around a closed belief system.

In the same sense, an individual cannot find 'God' when their belief system states 'there is definitely a God' without embracing the perspective that *there may not be a God.*

When one embraces *true knowing*, one does not simply know that there is a 'God' (or Source). One knows that consciousness seeks to know itself *therefore it may not be conscious.* If consciousness is not conscious then there cannot be Source or 'God'.

From this perspective, there is only the unknowing.

Yet unknowing becomes 'lack of knowledge' and therefore 'darkness' when it is not combined with knowing.

The merge of knowing and unknowing shines the light upon the darkness. What then emerges from this knowing/unknowing is love. For lovelight and lightlove are the natural products of the knowing/unknowing.

Manifestation of the Twin Flame Partner

When one moves into conscious manifestation of a twin flame partner upon Earth, one embraces *all perspectives.*

There is only one twin flame.

There is no twin flame.

There are many twin flames.

Everyone is my twin flame.

My higher self is my twin flame.

I am my higher self.

I am my own twin flame.

When one embraces these perspectives within knowing/unknowing, lightlove (confidence within the unknowing) and lovelight (knowing as a feeling, as a vibration), then one finds the 'tune' of the twin flame, if you will.

When one finds the tune of the twin flame, one *must* embrace the mirrored match in reality for that is how it works in a free will universe such as yours.

How Does One Find the Tune of the Twin Flame?

The tune of the twin flame is an emotion (emotions and sound are the same thing from our perspective).

The twin flame emotion is love. Therefore the *tune* of the twin flame is love.

Therefore *how do you find that love?* If you are not in a twin flame relationship, how can you find that love?

The love you are looking for is the love for Source, indeed it is the love for self.

3

As Above, So Below -

The Overworld and the Underworld

What happens if you don't love yourself? What can you do? Does this mean you will not manifest a twin flame relationship?

Finding love for self is very much crucial to the ascension or enlightenment journey. Finding this self-love is unique to each individual. Some may discover love for self after love for another (parent, romantic partner or child), yet it is said by many teachers in your spiritual field that *one cannot truly love another until one loves self.*

Indeed this is true, for love for self encompasses all, as love for self occurs within the enlightenment process. This does not mean that those who do not love self cannot love another, it means that the love they feel for the other will be conditional. This will be conditional based on the parameters of their own belief systems which will be shaped by their world view, experiences and level of integration of the shadow aspects.

When self-love takes place (coupled with the power of forgiveness and gratitude) then it is unconditional love that is embraced, experienced and expressed.

If you do not love yourself then (assuming you want to embrace love for self, this is always a choice for you have free will, yet your higher guidance, the 'codes within the matrix', will always be guiding you towards this self love), one would embark upon a healing journey in order to move into the shadow work necessary to integrate oneself within wholeness. One may call this shadow *work* yet when we use the word 'work' this is not to be interpreted in the negative (as in stressful and unwanted).

This work is such because it takes diligence, commitment and application, yet it is most important to see the aspect of this work that is fun!

Indeed it is challenging and can bring up many deep emotions that may mirror the original trauma as they are released, but there will always be a 'fun aspect' to this clearing given the huge relief and sense of accomplishment afforded oneself when this work is undertaken.

The twin flame relationship will manifest as a 'potential' if you have not found love for self, mirroring the love for self as a potential.

If love for self is not found within the individual's lifetime then so too will the twin flame relationship not be found. This is not to say that the partner of destiny will not be found or to say that a relationship is not available for that person.

If the potential for self-love is realised, so too will the potential for the twin flame relationship be realised.

How does the love for self and the twin flame relationship relate to the construction of the matrix/Mer-Ka-Bah field?

The twin flame, as we have said, is an 'energy' or 'consciousness' and the higher self aspect *is* the true twin flame. Within linear spatial awareness we find this higher self 'above oneself' if you will, within this vertical pillar of light formation.

The vertical pillar of light is the first step within a linear awareness of the matrix field and is the first aspect to 'build' or 'construct' on a conscious level.

When one constructs this matrix, beginning with the vertical pillar of light, one becomes aware of the 'as above, so below' and the significance of its meaning.

One becomes aware of the higher self, higher guidance, angelic aspect, ascended master realm, fifth dimension, heaven realities or the one true twin flame.

One moves higher within this vertical construct into other dimensions. One will specifically connect to the sixth dimension as the vertical pillar of light and thus the construction of the matrix is a sixth dimensional presentation of reality... although one is actually constructing a vehicle or transportation system that allows you to access all dimensions.

So when one thinks of the vertical pillar of light, one becomes aware of the vertical aspect of spatial awareness, as in up and down, higher than/lower than, ascending and descending.

Yet within the construction of the healthy matrix, moving downwards along this vertical pole does not necessarily equate to descension... only to movement and awareness of movement.

For as we have already said, one can reach the heaven dimensions/higher self/twin flame aspect by descending down the pole just as one ascends upwards.

Within a fifth dimensional awareness, the descension/ascension may be more aligned with the heaven/hell polarities, and certainly within a fourth dimensional construct this would be the case.

Yet when one embraces sixth dimensional awareness, the world of sacred geometry and mathematical equation, polarity is very different. Remember that the matrix, indeed the Mer-Ka-Bah, is *a sixth dimensional presentation in essence.*

Yet by virtue of the multidimensional light spectrum that it holds, the matrix/Mer-Ka-Bah is a key to accessing many dimensions. A vehicle or transportation system.

So within a fifth dimensional visual, one may see perhaps the beautiful meadow with one sacred building within that meadow, the crystal palace, guarded by unicorns or flying white horses like the Pegasus. This shamanic visualisation, an alphabetical numeral within the language of light, cosmic language system understood by the DNA, presents as the safe zone, safe place, hermetically sealed within the higher realms, the heaven realms. This would equate to the highermost points of the vertical pillar of light and would be 'that which is above you'. We could refer to this place as the fifth dimensional overworld.

Within a fifth dimensional visual of moving below oneself, sliding down the pole, if you will, and descending, one could perhaps find oneself within a dark forest. There may be one small wooden hut or little cottage within this forest, or one may make their home within the thick tree trunk of a magickal tree. The guardians here may be dragons, wolves, owls or elemental beings. If one has done shadow work to a high degree, one may not need to use the lower aspects of the vertical pole, that which we may call the fifth dimensional underworld.

Even when shadow work has been undertaken, one can still use this visual plane for magickal workings and manifestation.

Within a fifth dimensional presentation, one can visualise a lift or elevator. One steps into the elevator and sees two buttons. One saying 'OVERWORLD' or 'ABOVE', and the other saying 'UNDERWORLD' or 'BELOW'. One can choose to go upwards into the meadow with the crystal palace, or downwards into the dark forest.

For those who are wanting to work with shadow work and free themselves into the path of self love, this is a most aligned visual within the fifth dimensional field.

One would enter the lift, press the button for the underworld and descend downwards into the dark forest.

One would then ask for the manifestation of the shadow aspect to show itself so that you may communicate with it in order to unravel its meaning, identify it and integrate it.

Within our previous transmission, *Masters of the Matrix*, we spoke of emotional integration and the steps of *Acknowledgement, Gratitude, Analysis and Integration.*

These same steps are the ones to take with the manifestation of the shadow aspect that presents itself within your dark forest underworld reality. For you are ultimately working with an emotion here.

Remember that when you do this, you set the codes for *integration of the emotion* into your matrix field rather than the emotion itself.

Meditation, eyes open visualisation (the daydream) or actual dreamtime work are all appropriate platforms for the 'as above, so below' work which we speak of.

If going downwards in the elevator to the dark forest creates an uncomfortable emotion within you such as fear or anxiety, know that this is a most natural part of the process. For the human brain has created a defense mechanism by hiding the shadow trauma from you, so that you do not have to experience it and re-experience it over and over again.

We would advise working with a healer or practitioner in order to do this work if the anxiety or fear is too great for you. Having a facilitator with you as part of this work is most advised. Remember to treat this as an adventure, for surely it is that. This is what we mean when we say there is a 'fun aspect' to this work.

You can show this particular method of visualisation to your healer or facilitator and explain that you wish to visit the underworld/dark forest within a safe space. A practised hypnotherapist will be able to take you into this visualisation should that be the method you wish to use.

Or you can simply find a therapist you resonate with and follow their methods of shadow work. However this is done is your choice but know that this is part of the process of awakening, enlightenment and ascension.

The dark forest is a place of safety, even though you may naturally feel nervous of calling the manifestation of the shadow trauma to come to you. Gratitude will be your absolute key here, for no true service-to-self entity can continue to thrive in the presence of gratitude.

You may find that the landscape changes the minute you feel gratitude at the manifestation of the shadow trauma's visit. A rainbow may appear in the sky or one single pink rose may suddenly bloom amongst the dark forest floor. Or you may find yourself instantly transported to the overworld and the crystal palace within the meadow. If this happens then this is a sign that you are integrating spatial awareness of the vertical pillar of light, and that above and below are merging into the same place.

If you feel you can embark on this journey without another person present, then you can use the guardians within the dark forest as the facilitators. Whether they be dragons, wolves, owls or elemental beings... they are there for *you*. They are your best friends within the dark forest and they are there as your guardians.

Remember, gratitude is your key. You are absolutely thankful to the guardians and to the manifestation of the shadow trauma for coming to visit you in the dark forest.

Know also that the dragons and the presentations of the shadow traumas within the underworld are just as much your teachers as the unicorns and rainbow beings of light within the overworld are!

If you have worked extensively with the shadow aspect then you can utilise the dark forest/underworld for magickal workings and manifestation, and create this scenario as a fixed dreamtime template (a safe dream landscape you return to again and again) or use the elevator method to access the dark forest within the daydream or meditation.

You can set up an alter in your cottage or tree trunk home with candles, crystals and other personal objects of high magick. Really the sky is the limit here for you are working within the deep layers of your imagination, that which you would know as your 'field of creativity'. We, the White Winged Collective Consciousness of Nine, refer to this as 'hyperspace'.

The Overworld

The overworld is also a place for magickal workings and you can create a similar alter within your crystal palace.

If you link the overworld and the underworld to the energy centres of the human body, the chakras, then you would be working with the root, sacral and solar plexus chakras within the dark forest and the heart, throat and brow chakras (and somewhat the crown chakra) within the crystal palace in the meadow.

The overworld is the ideal place to connect to higher guidance and here all manner of higher dimensional beings can come to visit you to impart their teachings and wisdom.

This is also a most aligned place to access healing, for the crystal palace could be hexagonal-shaped and rays of healing light can pour into the palace through the different crystal hexagonal windows.

Or perhaps your crystal palace is dome-shaped but contains a healing room or spa that you visit regularly for deep healing treatments. Again, the sky is the limit... although in truth, it is not. For there are no limitations here in this magickal, visual world of your creating that stands as an alphabetical numeral of the language of light.

The shadow work, manifestation work, healing and higher connection all contribute to the formation of self-love.

For those individuals who have worked extensively within these visuals, working with the shadow and the higher reality, we may draw your attention back to the elevator. For you, in the elevator, there are three buttons now...

'OVERWORLD', 'UNDERWORLD' and 'MIDDLE WORLD'.

4

Middle World

and the Golden Triad of Ascension

Is Middle World this world? As in the third dimension? Why would we need a button in the elevator to get there if this is not a hyperspace/antimatter reality, but is here in this physical world?

The Middle World is the third dimension, yes. Yet there is an aspect to the third dimension that is not physically accessible as yet and is found within the hyperspace realms.

Within each dimension are other dimensions. In fact, there are layers of infinite dimensions within each dimension for the universal pattern is holographic and fractal... meaning it is infinitely divisible.

We refer to these 'mini dimensions' (if you will) as 'harmonics'.

Spirals Within Spirals

Within the third dimension (or more accurately, above the third dimension but below the fourth, in a linear sense, or even more accurately 'superimposed' within the fourth dimension, one could visualise this as 'spirals within spirals') is a harmonic that at one point was a physical presentation upon your planet. We could call this a 'realm' if you will, yet this that we speak of is that which the majority call 'a planet' upon your Earth.

This physical presentation (ultimately on a different timeline to your current Earth) was accessible within your past. It is your history, yet prior to what we would term 'known history' (that which the consciousness of humanity is aware of and/or believes to be reality).

This physical presentation is set to return to its accessibility (albeit in a different form) for all aware individuals within the third dimension. This harmonic shall be 'passed through' if you will, on your journey towards the higher dimensions.

Becoming aware of this harmonic that we would place betwixt the third and fourth dimensions (within the merge point or overlap) assists you to balance the architecture of the matrix as you become more and more aware of what you are!

You are an energy system, you *are* this matrix and you can experience whichever aspect of the geometry within the matrix that you desire to experience.

We show you the fifth dimensional presentation of these layers to the vertical pillar of light ('step one' within your spatial awareness regarding the construction of the matrix).

We remind you again, why are we assisting you to construct your matrix field? Because this brings awareness of the Mer-Ka-Bah which leads to activation of the Mer-Ka-Bah and the light body, and within this activation you begin to remember/know who and what you are. Then you will remember why you are here and what you are here to do.

Each one of you created a 'code' within your matrix field, an 'agreement' if you will, or contract.

The code can be translated as...

I will be provided with triggers, within my third dimensional reality, of the true reality so that I may remember my mission and access my mission at the physical level and the soul level.

All 'starseeds' hold this code. It is starseeds who shall find their way to this transmission and we are here to assist you starseeds in activating this code.

We do this through *Matrix Awareness, Matrix Mastery and Matrix Architecture.* We could perhaps refer to these three aspects as the 'Golden Triad of Ascension'.

For indeed we utilise the golden equation as you activate the bliss aspect, bliss charged love via the alchemical transformation of lovelight and lightlove, the triad of the three aspects of matrix memory triggers and light, the knowledge you accumulate as memory/knowings are activated. Therefore within this transmission you have the activation of the Golden Triad of Ascension.

So where is Middle World if not accessible within your physical dimension? This can be accessed via the elevator visualisation, standing as the central point within the vertical pillar of light and thus the central point of the matrix.

Whilst the central point of the matrix is indeed the zero point, the Middle World is the point you experience within the zero point. It is the true reality. This is the reality that once was and the reality you are returning to.

It is the reality of the fully formed crystalline DNA twelve strand formation, beyond the triple helix.

Your DNA activation into the crystalline matrix creates this reality, for the crystalline matrix is an awareness of consciousness. As you expand your awareness of consciousness and activate the DNA into this higher strand formation, this 'brings higher realities online' if you will.

The zero point, experienced through Middle World, is the crossover point between the vertical pillar of light (above and below) and the horizontal rainbow bridge pathway (past and future).

The vertical and the horizontal are, in the truest reality, in the same place, the same space. In order to become the Architect of the Matrix and construct the geometry needed, one needs to utilise spatial awareness within a linear sense. Therefore we have up and down (as above so below) and forward and backwards (future and past).

The point of connection, the crossover point (the central point of the formation that creates the sacred cross), would be known as the 'pivot point' or 'Middle World' (that which you experience in physical form).

Standing at the pivot point, one can see the pathway ahead, the pathway behind, the pathway above and the pathway below. One can also see the pathway to the left side of the pivot point and the pathway to the right side of the pivot point (the sideways arms of the sacred cross). These represent the quantum world, alternate selves and alternate timelines.

There are also diagonal aspects, coming in from the right and the left, creating the X shaped cross intersecting at the pivot point. The diagonal lines represent ancestral memories. There are other intersecting diagonal aspects within your matrix yet these are beyond the scope of this transmission at this time. They relate to 'harmonic time vectors' if you will. To translate this within a linear expression, these are 'ancestral memories' belonging to alternate aspects of self. This moves into a 'diagonal fractal' of information/knowing/memory of extraterrestrial ancestral memories on a linear and group soul level (moving into the quantum and multidimensional level). This entire grid complex is coming online for all starseeds as you activate the DNA codes of light.

This becomes natural, organic expansion into the spatial awareness of the matrix construction within the linear reality when DNA reconstruction/activation/creation takes place. Indeed, the awareness of the other infinities will come online collectively within your ascension process as you 'design this Matrix Architecture' if you will. Put another way, this will happen for you naturally as you remain open and receptive to the triggers.

Dreamwalker to Dreamweaver

We will explore further into the complexities and holographic fractalities of the matrix in more depth in future transmissions, as collectively your evolution within hyperspace takes you from dreamwalker to dreamweaver.

We shall bring forward more fractalised presentations of the matrix through our conduit, yet at this point she learns in this step by step method that we present to you. She wants to know much and quickly and you, starseeds of Gaia, indeed we see that you are the same! We say to our conduit as we say to you, one must walk before one can run. If one learns this way, with patience, one indeed shall fly!

The first step is that one must become rooted within the familiarity of the vertical pillar of light and the pivot point/Middle World. One cannot expand into the fractality with full awareness unless the original building blocks are there. The 'foundations' if you will. Therefore trust your own process within the construction of the divine architecture. If full awareness and processing of the divine architecture is desired by you, then we recommend the step by step method which we speak of. The starting point here is the vertical pillar of light and the pivot point. The crystalline activation cannot move back into a descension pattern once the original pillar is constructed. Once 'firmly in your mind' if you will, it shall remain. Remember, you who stand as starseeds are moving into a 'reconstruction' rather than a construction. You already hold this awareness within your fields for you incarnated on planet Earth with intact memory codes. Therefore all we present here is *a reminder of that which you already know.*

In order to truly understand Middle World and what this represents for humanity's future, one needs to know what this used to represent.

For you as a planet, as you approach completion, shall return to what once was, but in a different form. For this is the journey of Source.

So what exactly did Middle World represent? For this we must go back into Earth's past, beyond your known history, and start, as they say, 'at the beginning'.

5

The Original Seeding of Earth

In your last transmission "Masters of the Matrix", you mentioned 'ancient codes for a new dawn of man'. You said the realisation of these 'codes' is an alchemical process.

Can you explain what this means?

'Ancient codes' refers to 'codes' within the cellular matrix (the DNA) of each human incarnate being on Earth. These 'codes' were placed within your DNA thousands and thousands of years ago at the very beginning of your creation. This was the time when 'man' and 'extraterrestrial' fused together, if you will.

We could also say that this was the time when the higher aspect of self and the physical aspect of self 'separated' (in truth there was no separation, yet this is perceived as such within the third dimension).

When you say 'fused together', do you mean that extraterrestrials had children with the humans?

Not exactly... this was more of an 'energy transfer' if you will, where the hominid beings on Earth were infused with the matrix codes and the light of the extraterrestrials energy blueprint. One could call this 'advanced genetic engineering'.

The matrix codes then reproduced within offspring of the original hominid and became part of the evolution of humanity. Therefore we can truthfully say that all of humanity are 'descendants' of extraterrestrials and are indeed seen as 'their children'.

How were these codes placed within our DNA?

This was part of the energetic transfer. We would need to explain about light here in order to respond to your question fully.

The best way to show you what happened here is to speak in metaphor. Imagine, if you will, one small animal. Let us use the example of a rabbit. If 'light' is beamed upon that rabbit in the right way, in the right intensity, it will 'feed new codes' into the rabbit's DNA. The rabbit, through evolution, will then begin to transform into a new type of animal. This may take thousands of years, yet the changes will begin in that rabbit and in the rabbit's offspring. This is a metaphor for how these codes were placed within your DNA. Through 'light transfer' if you will.

The light we speak of is not simply electric light or even sunlight (although sunlight is nearer to the light we are explaining). Perhaps we could refer to this as 'cosmic light'.

Let us then look closer at this cosmic light. As you look closer you will begin to see geometric formations within this light. We could refer to this as a 'monadic light template.'

These geometric formations are light codes themselves, yet they are also beings. Living intelligent beings. They are pure 'intelligent energy' in themselves and they are creators. These beings are the light. They ARE the DNA codes. In fact, one could refer to them as DNA itself or indeed the templates for 'planetary DNA seeding' for this is what they are!

One could call them angels. Or extraterrestrials. Both would be correct. These angels, extraterrestrials, light codes, monads/monadic entities or intelligent energies live inside each and every one of you.

Now we may move further into this 'story'.

There are different kinds of these living light codes. Different geometric formations within the light.

Each geometric formation, whilst made up of the same 'building blocks' if you will, are unique. Each time they replicate themselves (by beaming their light onto the rabbit - you - in order to transfer their codes to you), each resulting creation from their replication is unique. And that is you, you are a unique presentation of these geometric light codes.

Why did the hominid beings not have these codes in the first place?

The hominid beings were 'creations of the Earth' if you will. They grew from the original DNA seeding upon your planet. Each planet is naturally seeded with DNA. So indeed they did have codes. Unique codes based on natural organic DNA template seeding. This is the 'human template' if you will, and it can grow from any structure. Each 'planet' or 'colony' will be unique in its seeding, yet the human template, the original construct for DNA expression, is the same.

So codes were indeed there yet they were 'accelerated' if you will.

DNA is beamed throughout the universes and galaxies, every particle or atom or space or non-space is 'teeming with life'. Everything exists in a state of potential.

When your planet Earth began to form, the DNA was seeded upon your planet as is the natural order of things. The natural way. After many billions of years of creation, the hominid beings came into being.

This creational aspect upon your planet is the process of the first and second density of existence. The geometric beings of light came forward to 'speed up', if you will, the progression from second density into third density.

This can be viewed as 'infiltration' from one perspective, yet from another perspective it is seen as assistance. This is a complex and challenging situation for most humans to grasp given the high levels of compassion for 'other' that you hold. The 'infiltration' is not easy to comprehend and it is even less so when 'assistance' is also a truthful perspective. If you are able to embrace more than one concept at the same time and you can see the 'paradoxes' within reality constructs, then you will have no difficulty in processing this information.

Ascension Blueprint

For those who cannot yet do this (and you will be able to in time, given the journey you are on and the activation that is taking place), we would recommend bringing in boundaries, strength and determination regarding infiltration (and forgiveness once you are able to move into this), and gratitude regarding assistance. Yet we would say to you to embrace these emotional feelings (for they are codes, they are templates and they are programmable... they have outcomes) with neutrality or as close to neutrality as you can. Not the indifference or uncaring neutrality but the 'observer viewpoint' objective neutrality. This is the emotional template you are looking for that is the code that stands in alignment with the crystalline DNA formation. The 'crystal palace within hyperspace' or the 'Emerald City of Krysta'. We present the metaphor for your decoding. This metaphor/symbol/language of light decoding is becoming easier and easier as you activate more and more filaments within the crystalline lattice that is humanity's 'ascension blueprint'.

The Call

'A call' will always be put out from the life within one density to the life within the higher densities for 'assistance'.

What is actually happening is a merging.

The beings from the higher densities 'merge' with the beings within the lower (or denser) densities in order to continue to create, experience and learn.

Sometimes second density beings come to 'a standstill' if you will (meaning they are not moving forward within their evolution). A forward moving motion, that which we call 'momentum', is essential for the growth of every soul.

When the 'second density call' was put out, several different beings (different geometric formations) were then free to come forward and answer the call.

At first, only service-to-others polarity geometric formations came forward to 'deliver their light codes' to the hominid beings on Earth. Earth was to be 'a grand experiment', to be 'unique'.

Earth is known as 'the jewel', not only in your universe but in many other universes. There are many of these 'jewel' planets, but Earth was a very unique planetary experiment. Why? Because several different types of geometric light code formations assisted in seeding their light into the hominid beings of Earth. This created somewhat of a diversity, rare for most newly transitioning third density planets.

It was decided that Earth's 'children' or 'creations' would be given every chance to progress through momentum. Therefore the 'children of Earth' (original hominid Earth beings merged with the geometric light code formations of living energetic intelligence) were to be free to choose how they would utilise momentum. The law of free will template, through the law of one unity template, was placed within the planetary grid structures in accordance with universal and galactic law.

These newly birthed third density 'children' needed to experience contrast in order to experience free will and choice. They needed to have something to 'choose between', so polarity was created upon Earth. The 'polarity templates' were also placed within the planetary grid structures.

In a manner of speaking, we then say that some 'children of Earth' were further 'interfered with' or 'assisted' by giving them different 'flavours', if you will, of this light. Different light codes.

The polarisation that then formed upon the newly birthed third density Earth was that of positive polarisation, negative polarisation and 'shades of grey' in-between, if you will, with a central neutrality OR unpolarised energy available also.

There was therefore much choice leading to free will expression and an accelerated growth and expansion 'accelerated momentum' upon Earth.

We can add further to this 'story'.

Each living energetic intelligence/geometric light code formation of DNA was answering the second density call within alignment, regardless of polarisation. As in 'free will' was respected. This is universal and galactic law on a quantum level. This *was* respected. This was the 'order of things' shall we say, for many aeons of time. Much creation and change took place.

The 'children of Earth' were most 'interesting' shall we say, to a great many other DNA seeded races of beings due to the fact that very 'high vibrational' geometric light code formations were the original 'transformers' of the second density Earth hominids.

These light codes are never lost, they are always replicated. Earth was quite unique in that a second density planet was 'seeded' (through the energetic genetic manipulation) by very advanced, higher dimensional frequencies as well as many other diverse frequencies.

An Unknown Quantity

How this would 'play out' for beings upon the newly birthed Earth was an unknown quantity, even within the quantum universes and through timelines that had already experienced the 'outcomes' (your potential futures).

The third density beings on Earth held activated light codes. They knew who they were and they held memories of the 'original seed', as in 'of Source'. They all knew they were Source.

They could do 'amazing' things such as telepathy, bilocation, levitation, telekinesis and teleportation. They understood and could utilise various

91

forms of alchemy. They could 'leave their bodies' at will and travel to other planetary systems and dimensions in what you would know as 'their astral bodies'. They knew how to activate their Mer-Ka-Bah. They were each such beautiful beings of light, and the majority of them chose to polarise within the positive vibration.

Garden of Eden

Those who chose to polarise within the negative were respectful of the positive and vice versa. They considered themselves brothers and sisters and there were very few disagreements amongst the 'children of Earth' despite their different polarisations. This is difficult to understand from the perspective you have within such a densely polarised reality such as yours. Suffice it to say, that the polarisation within this 'Garden of Eden' was a much lighter presentation of negative/positive polarity therefore expressed and received quite differently to the polarisation you experience in third dimensional Earth.

Yet many aeons into Earth's third density development, other beings came to Earth. These beings were of service-to-self. Some of these beings were within free will boundaries as they had been 'called' by service-to-self negative polarised beings on Earth *for there must always be a call.*

Yet there were other service-to-self beings who did not wait for a call. They went beyond the boundaries of the free will laws in order to infiltrate. They did this in order to assist the third density beings to polarise, giving them more contrast, more free will and faster, more accelerated momentum. The trade-off regarding this perceived 'gift' to the children of Earth was that they would have a far larger 'playing field' if you will, in which to create their own negative polarised density with negative polarised planets.

There are several levels to this. At the one level this infiltration/assistance was fully decided by both polarities when both those polarities were one.

One being 'split itself' if you will, in order to 'play the game of expansion upon the playground of Earth'.

Yet from a different level, this was infiltration and was against free will boundaries. *An 'agreement was broken' if you will.*

This situation has remained throughout the development of Earth's third density. From one perspective, it is an 'agreement' (from the same being that split itself into two polarities). From another perspective, it is an infiltration that would only resolve when humanity put out another call.

When the call is put out, then this signifies that the planet is ready for ascension/graduation. This will mean a shift into a new density. When humanity put out the call (the call being triggered by the infiltration/assistance), it meant that humanity and planet Earth were ready to transition from third density into fourth density.

Once 'the call' reached critical mass point, then the transition from third density to fourth density would begin.

This is the stage you are at now in your evolution as a planet. You are currently 'in transition' and have been for some time.

This is why we are here (along with many other galactic guardians or guidance structures).

You see, we are the geometric light code formations that seeded your planet all those aeons ago when your planet was in second density. The reason why we are those geometric light code formations is because we are an exact replica of the original geometric light code formations. We are contained within each and every structure on Earth. We manifest as exact replicas of the original light codes within third density humans who are ready to transition into the fourth density.

We are the DNA. We are the DNA of our conduit, yet we are the DNA of every human being on Earth. Within some, the light codes lay dormant. In fact, within many they lay dormant. Yet within many, they are activated.

A very interesting situation takes place once the geometric light codes within the DNA begin to activate. They do exactly what we had originally hoped they would do. *They radiate.*

Meaning they spread, they are catching. Earth is unique in that she is a garden of light. Each human being on Earth is capable of radiating the same light as the original seeds of light.

The original geometric light code formations have replicated within you, creating, if you will, a 'body of light'. You are able to radiate the light to others just as the original light codes radiated their light to you.

This can, of course, be achieved via a positive polarisation or a negative polarisation.

We speak to you from the positive polarisation, as our conduit has polarised within the positive which makes 'us' positive.

Or perhaps we could say, we radiated our positive polarised light to her and she 'caught' it, creating a positive polarisation within her being. All is the same and both occur simultaneously.

6

Giants, Lilliputians and Elementals

How is this story connected to 'Middle World' and the construction of the matrix?

Middle World, the physically manifested experience that the incarnated human individual creates for himself or herself, would currently be your third dimension that you exist within now.

Yet your current Middle World experience is a mirrored representation of the double helix DNA structure that calls unto itself the third dimensional, linear experience within matter.

What Middle World used to represent was quite different from your current linear experience. Middle World, prior to your known history, was a manifested projection of the full twelve stranded DNA crystalline structure and therefore the experience of the physical reality was a reflection of the crystalline structure.

The Infinite Helix

We speak here in terms of the full twelve stranded pattern, and yet there were quantum projections of this. In truth the presentation of the DNA field exists within an 'infinite helix' if you will, and within matter (of varying degrees of frequency). We could pinpoint 144,000 strands of the DNA sequence.

Yet looking within linear understanding of this quantum aspect, we speak here in simplified terms. Hence we use the presentation of the twelve stranded DNA helix formation.

So what kind of reality did the twelve strand crystalline structure manifest?

The reality manifested was a direct vibrational match to the consciousness held by the beings on Earth at that time. These beings, in their innocence (as total reflections of the innocence of original Source) were presentations of breathtaking beauty. They were human, like you, and many looked exactly as you look now, yet others had differences. Many had wings and are what you would now term as 'elemental beings'.

You could say that 'humans and elementals lived side by side' or that 'the portals to the elemental realm remained open'. Both of these statements would be correct. Yet in the truest reality, these winged creates *were* human. Just different kinds of human beings.

There were so many different forms of physical structure at that time. Some of these humans were incredibly large by your standards. You would know these as 'giants', yet they were simply human. Like you.

Some of these humans were very, very small. As tiny as the Lilliputians in your famous story *Gulliver's Travels.*[*]

Within your fictional writings, under the genres of fantasy, science fiction or surrealism, there are many truths to be found. We again draw your attention to the importance of 'the story'.

These humans, due to having the higher crystalline DNA formation, could communicate with each other without speech. They could 'step in and out' of a 'groupmind' if you will. This groupmind is that which we would describe as a 'telepathic and empathic union' rather than the 'hive mind control system' that is the presentation of service-to-self energy.

The telepathic and empathic union was a unification of consciousness that the crystalline beings could choose to access at will.

Another way of describing this would be to say that they could access the 'Akashic records' or the 'Halls of Amenti' whenever they pleased.

These humans lived within the 'harmonics' of the third dimension. There was far more unity within the third dimensional harmonic scale as opposed to the separation within your third dimension now (although this is now changing).

Once There Were Dragons

Within Middle World were animals that were also quite different to the animals that exist within your third dimensional Earth now. There were birds, reptiles and felines that were very different, similar to your legends and myths of dragons and griffins.

---

[*]   *Gulliver's Travels* by Jonathan Swift

If you were to imagine a world from one of your fictional fantasy stories with magick, fairies, pixies, giants, dragons and unicorns, then this would be somewhat of a similar presentation to the Middle World that we speak of. You may think of these beings as fantastic creatures that are so very beyond anything within actual 'reality', yet these beings are simply humans like you and animals just like the animals you have on your planet now. They were simply different.

They could bilocate and multilocate (be in two or more places at once), although this is not as literal as it seems. This action was more of an ability to project their consciousness forward into two different places at once or several places at once, and for other beings to recognise them and then communicate and interact with them (rather than them moving their actual physical body). There are individuals upon your planet now who can do this and are doing this.

There were many more differences within these humans, and if we were to say to you that this was a 'world filled with magick', this would be accurate given humanity's interpretation of magick. However, this was natural to them, it was the way the world was.

The Elemental Realm

There are many intuitive and sensitive individuals upon your planet now. We would call these individuals 'starseeds', those that have had visions of this Middle World of which we speak. These starseeds would know of this place as 'the elemental realm'.

Indeed some of these 'visions' which the starseeds hold of this Middle World presentation are exactly that. Windows into a reality that once was (and exists within the quantum stream), accessible via remote viewing, clairvoyance and astral travel within the dreamtime.

Yet for a great many of these starseeds, these are not simply visions. *They are memories.*

We speak here on a linear level for all humanity will have cellular memory of all and everything (albeit dormant/buried memory).

On a linear level, many starseeds have had incarnations within the time period prior to your known history and within the Middle World presentation we speak of. It would also be correct to say that many starseeds are aware of their 'alternate selves' and will have direct knowing of (and often communication with) the alternate self that currently experiences the reality that is Middle World. They will know of the aspect of self that exists as an elemental, giant, fairy, pixie or similar being.

So what happened? Why are these elemental beings no longer in third dimensional reality?

When humanity experienced 'the fall', their crystalline DNA structure changed. The codons for multidimensionality and memory were 'switched off', 'lost' or 'stolen' (all explanations correct depending on vantage point).

In order for souls to individualise and present experience to the original Source (we speak here on a linear level therefore Source presents as original Source of innocence), souls had to go forth and discover and make known the unknown. This was so that original Source could know itself and thus know all and everything and become all knowing. On a linear level, Source moves from the beginning point of original Source of innocence to the end point of all-knowing. In truth this is a simultaneous point of existence, singularity or pulse.

The presentation of Middle World from a more restricted DNA formation created a material or fabric of reality in alignment with the consciousness of humanity.

This was not something that occurred overnight. A 'descension' down the frequencies occurred over time. Evolution (moving down the spiral) created more and more beings that 'forgot' who they were. They could no longer join the telepathic and empathic union or access the 'Halls of Amenti', therefore they no longer realised that the reality they experienced was a complete holographic presentation of their unified thought structure. They no longer realised they lived within an illusion. *They believed their reality to be real.*

However, not all of these beings completely lost their memories. Many of those who remained within memory were service-to-self beings. A minority few were service-to-others beings. Whilst they too lost the crystalline structure (for the fabric of reality could no longer support the crystalline structure), they retained a higher memory formation and did not fully descend into the double helix.

The Inner Earth Kingdoms

The majority of the service-to-self beings retreated into underground dwellings and caves within that which you would know as 'the inner Earth kingdoms'.

Yet there was always an intention to switch from descension to ascension and begin again an upward climb. Or we could say, there would come a time when humanity would regain what has been taken from them. *This time is now.*

7

Jewel Planet and the Nine Triads of the Matrix

You mentioned that Earth was known as 'the jewel' or a 'jewel planet'. Why is this?

This word we use - 'jewel' - is an energetic translation. The energetic we would bring forward here to explain your Earth is 'one of beauty and riches', indeed 'a prize of the highest order' and the word 'jewel' fits the energetic translation.

The Earth regenerates at a rapid rate. Earth holds a high ability to birth lush forests, mountainous and rocky land and crystal clear waters in abundance.

DNA has seeded itself well on Earth. There are other reasons that Earth is seen as such a 'prize' if you will, yet these are reasons that are based on the service-to-self need for sustenance and this involved humanity itself, not just the planet.

From a service-to-others perspective, Earth is seen as a jewel due to her abundant beauty and ability to replenish herself so rapidly. Yet also from that perspective, we could perhaps see Earth as 'the little sister' in a family of only brothers. She is to be nurtured and protected. She is as a 'rose amongst the thorns' if you will, and the love that is held for her is absolute.

She is known by other names. Many extraterrestrial races would know your home planet as 'Gaia' or 'Terra'.

How can you take back the memory codes that were stolen from you? Were they taken because of Earth being a jewel planet?

Many of the individuals known as 'starseeds' are already taking back or regaining/restructuring the memory codes. Many are teaching (with the help of the guardians and higher guidance) how to move into this regaining/restructuring process. This is our teaching here and the reason for this transmission.

The answer to your second question is yes, from a third and fourth dimensional perspective, the memory codes were taken because service-to-self groups coveted the prize of the jewel planet, your Earth.

Beyond the fourth dimension, the reasons for 'the fall' no longer align with anyone or anything 'taking' or 'stealing' anything from you. From the higher dimensional perspective, these were free choices made by the 'you' that encompasses the Logos/demiurge/spirit-deity god/Central Sun aspect of Source presentation.

You made the decision to move into descension, and full or partial amnesia, in order to individualise as a matrix/soul construct and to present the original Source innocence aspect with the original Source all-knowing aspect.

You have incarnated into a physical reality with 'dormant codes' if you will, within your cellular structure, within your DNA.

These dormant codes are memory codes and when they 'activate', your memory returns.

The memory that returns to you is perceived differently depending on which dimensional field you are 'viewing' the memory from.

Or one could say, depending on which 'strand' of your DNA is activated. In truth, these are one and the same.

One could label these memories within, that of third, fourth and fifth dimensions. One could label the perspectives in the sense of your own personal energy centres which move into a 'cosmic formation' if you will. Meaning they are viewed from different 'cosmic coordinates' such as celestial, solar and galactic.

The celestial (being the level of the stars often referred to as 'the stellar gateway', this is presented here as the violet ray or the silver ray).

Solar (the level of Earth's sun, this is presented here as the golden and silver rays).

Galactic (the level of the Grand Central Sun, also known as the 'Logos', this is presented here as the platinum ray).

There are many models to explain this raise in consciousness, and different connected conduits on your planet use different terminologies. What is more, they use the same terminologies to refer to different aspects and this can be confusing for the seeker.

We would suggest that you find a model which you resonate with, that seems to be a concept that is simple for you to grasp rather than complicated or confusing.

Ultimately your own model (that which comes to you through communications, dreams and intuitions) is the model for you to work with.

Here we present the model that resonates most closely with our conduit and therefore human individuals who hold similar perceptions of metaphors and emotional fields to our conduit.

If one visualises the chakras, as one knows them in the most widely used model...

Base/Root - Red

Sacral - Orange

Solar Plexus - Yellow

Heart - Green (or Pink)

Throat - Blue

Third Eye/Brow - Indigo

Crown - Violet (or White)

Imagine then, that there is another chakra, belonging to you, part of your energy body, at the level of the stars. This is indeed the truth. Suggested colour to visualise would be silver.

Visualise another chakra, belonging to you, part of your energy body, at the level of the sun. This is also indeed the truth. Suggested colour to visualise would be gold.

Then imagine, if you will, a further chakra, belonging to you, part of your energy body, at the level of the centre of the galaxy. Again, this is truth. Suggested colour to visualise would be platinum (or visualise a diamond within this chakra point).

Whilst this is a simplified model regarding your energetic connection to your solar system, universe and entire cosmos, it is a model that is in alignment with the accuracy of how things truly are for you.

Each of these chakra points - celestial, solar and galactic - are perspectives of reality. Perspectives of self, the true self that is you. For you are the absolute reflection of these higher perspectives. These aspects are your consciousness and within each aspect memories are contained. Memories that belong to you and the experiences that you have as a soul.

The Galactic Stargates

You said to visualise a diamond at the centre of the galaxy, the galactic core, as another chakra, part of our energy body, which will connect our matrix to the galactic core. Yet I have been told that the galactic core is actually a black hole. I was also told that if we take our matrix through a black hole, this will lead us into a reality system that is a trap, bringing us back into the reincarnational cycle against our will. This could mean that we will once again lose our memories and descend or fall back into the double helix, linear reality and would not be able to ascend with the crystalline DNA formation. Please can you tell me if this is true?

This is a very good question. In order to respond to this, one would visualise a multidimensional universe in a 'layer' type system. Let us refer to these as 'lower layers' and 'higher layers', which are simplified presentations of the true reality which is fractal and infinite. The true 'layers' are actually spirals superimposed upon/inside other spirals. For ease of explanation, we will look here at layers.

Your galaxy has 'lower layers' and 'higher layers' within it. The lower layers are those of matter and the higher layers are those of antimatter (a simplified explanation of the true presentation for antimatter exists through all dimensions and matter/antimatter is merged).

Your galactic core is a 'multidimensional stargate'. It is an intersection of many 'highways and byways' if you will.

Your sun is also a stargate, as are many points at the celestial (star) level.

When you 'travel' within your energy body/Mer-Ka-Bah/matrix, it will depend on the level of activation/light quotient that you hold as to 'where you go', should you decide to travel through any of these stargates.

The destination is a direct match to your state of consciousness and awareness.

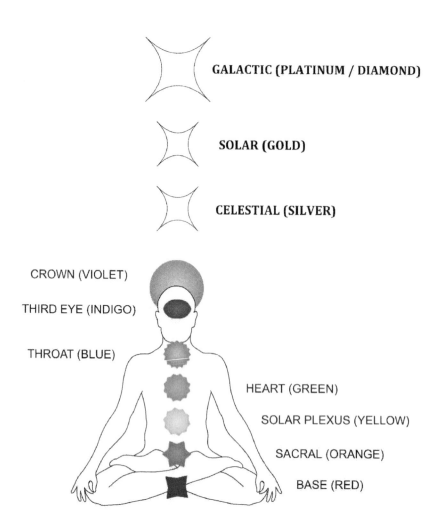

GALACTIC (PLATINUM / DIAMOND)

SOLAR (GOLD)

CELESTIAL (SILVER)

CROWN (VIOLET)

THIRD EYE (INDIGO)

THROAT (BLUE)

HEART (GREEN)

SOLAR PLEXUS (YELLOW)

SACRAL (ORANGE)

BASE (RED)

Above: The ten chakra model

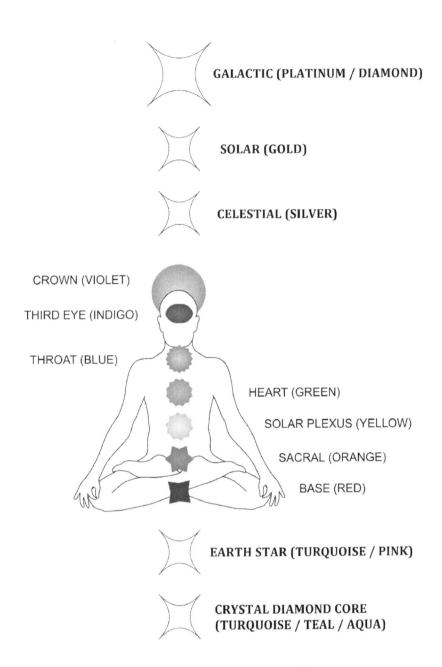

GALACTIC (PLATINUM / DIAMOND)

SOLAR (GOLD)

CELESTIAL (SILVER)

CROWN (VIOLET)

THIRD EYE (INDIGO)

THROAT (BLUE)

HEART (GREEN)

SOLAR PLEXUS (YELLOW)

SACRAL (ORANGE)

BASE (RED)

EARTH STAR (TURQUOISE / PINK)

CRYSTAL DIAMOND CORE
(TURQUOISE / TEAL / AQUA)

Above: The twelve chakra model

ABOVE THE GALACTIC CHAKRA AND BELOW THE CRYSTAL DIAMOND CORE ARE THE MAGENTA AND THE EMERALD RAYS THAT BEGIN THE UNIFICATION OF THE CHAKRAS INTO THE RAINBOW LIGHT.

The lower layers within your galaxy equate to denser consciousness levels and the higher layers equate to higher consciousness levels.

Again, we draw your attention to the fact that this is a very simplified presentation of a most complex, multidimensional and quantum system. When you travel this way, you are not moving through space; you are moving through time.

Space and time are actually one and the same from our perspective and are simply interchangeable mirrors to one another. In your linear reality, they are experienced very differently.

Therefore within these lower layers of your galaxy, all that you say is correct. The centre of your galaxy is a black hole and if you were to travel through this black hole, in your Mer-Ka-Bah/matrix as an externalised energy system without holding the charge/light quotient/crystalline DNA strand formation needed for 'acceleration' shall we say, then one would indeed move into the reincarnational trapping system you mention.

We speak of this somewhat within our previous transmission, *Masters of the Matrix*.

These lower layers of your galaxy equate to the fourth dimensional fields and the infinite fractal, harmonic realities within the fourth dimension.

The higher galactic layers equate to the fifth dimension and beyond. Travelling through the galactic core within these layers would not take you into a reincarnational trapping system, for this does not exist beyond the fourth dimension. One would 'bypass' the trapping system and move into a system that is part of an ascension matrix.

However, when activating the Mer-Ka-Bah/matrix, one does not need to transport oneself in a linear fashion.

On your planet, ships move along the sea in a linear fashion. Space travel within the third dimension would also move this way. You may see the movement of ships this way within your science-fiction/science-fantasy stories.

The activated Mer-Ka-Bah/matrix would work instantaneously when piloted by the experienced meditator/dreamwalker/Master of the Matrix.

One simply visualises 'where' one wants to go and, with the correct crystalline patterning, one will find oneself within a consciousness reality structure that mirrors the patterning within the DNA fields created by your directed, intentional visualisation.

Our transmissions are brought through our conduit for this very reason. They are to assist you into your own memories and knowings of how to create the crystalline patterning needed to traverse galaxies, stargates and cosmic highways and byways. You are master of your reality when you hold the pattern of knowing.

Placing a diamond within the galactic core instantly transfers all energy systems within all that is you, throughout the quantum field into the pattern of the higher layers of your galaxy and connects you to a multIdimensional stargate that leads to the reality match of all that you are.

The lovelight/lightlove into bliss charged love creates the golden mean frequency within the DNA fields, which hold the charge and the pattern of the diamond template within the galactic core chakra aspect. When this golden/diamond charge is created through the alchemy that is linear double helix into crystalline infinite helix, *it is not possible to fall into a trapping system of any kind.*

When you travel through a 'stargate', the destination depends on your crystalline template, and the charge created from it, in order to move you into what we would call 'acceleration' (light speed momentum).

Acceleration (light speed momentum) can only occur within the higher layers of any galactic system, and there are no trapping systems within those realities.

The teachings presented within these transmissions directly relate to you creating the acceleration (light speed momentum) within your Mer-Ka-Bah matrix, and this is directly related to the crystalline DNA matrix and the cellular memory structure.

All visuals, language of light alphabetical numerals and frequency keys within our transmissions are there to trigger you into these crystalline memory formations.

The diamond chakra link with the galactic core/multidimensional stargate is one such trigger.

We understand that there is much information presented to you coming in from many different sources at this time on your planet. We refer to this as 'the deluge'. Indeed, it is the prophesied 'flood' that we speak of. This is both a flood of energy and a flood of information as many pathways within your DNA structure come online.

When perceiving within third/fourth dimensional perspectives, then much of the higher dimensional information can elicit confusion and fear.

Confusion can be positive in the sense that it can lead to clarity, for it pushes you into momentum and the seeking of that which will unravel the confusion.

Yet it can be negative if it remains for an extended period of time, without momentum and when intertwined with fear.

If this is the case for you, then we would direct you to our previous transmission *Masters of the Matrix* and the emotional integration methods we speak of.

Fear and confusion are created through lack of knowing (or lack of confidence in one's knowing).

When information is delivered to you (especially during the time that is the deluge, your 'now') from he or she who speaks with confidence and authority about a subject you do not know or understand, then it is easy to take the knowledge or information from that individual as fact or absolute truth.

Yet absolute truth cannot be delivered to you from another person (or higher dimensional being through another physical person). You can only access this through your own searching, seeking, activation, memory and knowing.

All you can gain from another is their unique perspective.

We would include ourselves and our conduit within this. Take 'truth' from naught but self. Learn to 'resonate' within the balance that is your own fractalised divine architecture. It is this that we present within our transmissions. Activations, NOT absolutes.

Therefore, we say seek far and wide and look to all places. Dismiss that which is not a match within your fields and retain that which is.

Here in this transmission, you will find the tools within which to do this. Whilst we present information, it is a perspective, a tool, indeed a gift. It can be utilised in many ways.

To conclude regarding this issue, we would describe this information as *matrix memory triggers for ascension.*

The Veil of Forgetfulness

So let us look here at memory.

The current situation regarding incarnation on your planet is such that when you incarnate into a physical body, the 'veil of forgetfulness' is laid over your eyes, if you will. You move into an incarnation with no conscious memory of what has gone before, or even of what you are.

As you grow as an infant, you begin to retain memory. Yet still you have not fully individualised as an independent physical human being, for you see yourself as at one with Source. For your 'memory' of Source and your unity of Source, your very beingness of Source, is all that you have.

As you grow, you begin to acquire individualisation as a human being and experience what it is to be separate from Source.

You then live out your linear experience in a physical reality and when you leave that incarnation, you return to a non-physical state, retaining both individualisation and unity simultaneously (for your perception is no longer a linear one). From that vantage point, you can re-evaluate the physical experience you have just undertaken in that lifetime.

You can then plan out which further experience would most best serve you as a soul.

This is the 'standard experience' that most shall undergo as a physical being.

Yet there comes a time when each planet, and the beings upon that planet, begin to 'turn back towards the light' if you will. They 'yearn' for the unity they once experienced, and they wish to experience this within a physical reality.

This triggers the 'call' if you will, or the 'template' for the experience you know as 'ascension'.

It is the experience where memory returns to the individual whilst in physical incarnation. The individual does not need to leave the physical incarnation in order for these memories to return.

The linear experience of memory is where experience is retained and not forgotten. Even within linear experience, it is extremely rare for an incarnated individual to remember every experience throughout their lifetime. Memory comes in sections. The whole is not seen at once but the sections are seen individually and non-sequentially whenever the desire to look at them is there.

Three Triads of Mind

The conscious mind takes note of experience, yet so too does the subconscious mind. We can perhaps see memory as three triads of mind.

The first triad would be that of conscious memory, the memory of every experience your conscious mind has accumulated. This first triad is the linear experience and where the majority of incarnated humans are upon your planet Earth in their thinking.

The second triad would be that of subconscious memory. The memory of what has been on the periphery of your conscious mind.

For example, let us take Jonathan, a six-year-old boy, to explain the second triad of memory.

Jonathan is asleep. He is dreaming of being on a beach with birds flying around him. His subconscious mind is 'in control' if you will, whilst his conscious mind takes 'a rest'.

Jonathan's parents are watching television in the next room. The television is on a loud setting, enough for Jonathan to hear. Yet he does not react to or process any of the information coming in from the television show, for he is asleep and he is dreaming. His 'focus' if you will, is on the dream.

The television show is about a fictitious paradisical island. Let us call this island 'Sunnisea Island' for the purposes of this example.

Jonathan has never heard the term 'Sunnisea Island' before or since this moment.

Twenty years later, Jonathan starts to think about a mythical paradise by the name of Sunnisea Island, and he imagines a story centred around this island. He then discovers the film (that his parents were watching twenty years previously) with the exact same story that he, himself imagined. He wonders how on Earth this can be possible and thinks perhaps he is 'psychic'.

Indeed he would be correct for many 'psychics' use a blend of second and third triad memory. The second triad is the memory from the periphery of the conscious mind. That is the memory triad that Jonathan had activated when he started to imagine the story of Sunnisea Island.

Psychic individuals are no different from non-psychic individuals. They have simply learned to use a different part of their brain. The aspect responsible for peripheral memory or second triad memory.

What then is the third triad of memory? This is the memory field that contains the 'memories' of all individuals that have ever lived upon the planet you have incarnated upon. This would be akin perhaps to the lower floors of the Akashic library. This is a dimension where all memory of experience is contained. This is also the 'fourth dimension'.

This is also the same dimension where 'spirit' reside (spirit simply being memory fields of individuals that once existed in physical form who have continued their linear experience in a non-physical form, anchored by the thought and the consciousness of those still living in physical human form).

Psychics think with this third triad of memory. They are therefore able to access the memories of any being that has ever existed upon the planet at any time (although this process may be linear, depending on the individual, as in they access just one being's memory, yet this is still 'outside' their own conscious experience within their current lifetime).

These three triads of memory have always been available upon your planet for each incarnated individual to experience and they are 'normal' memory fields, if you will (even though the scientists upon your planet have still not yet validated any memory field beyond the first triad).

Some of your scientists experiments are indeed 'proving' the second triad, if you will, but the third triad of memory remains firmly rooted in your arena of philosophy, (specifically metaphysics) at this time.

Is DNA activation needed for second and third triad memory?

In many ways, the second triad of memory activation is part of the 'normal' memory pathway of any individual. It simply is not practised or understood well enough, yet it is indeed part of being a physical third dimensional human being. However, there is a slight activation within the DNA strands when the second triad of memory is accessed. There is a slight change in brainwaves. This would be akin to being in a light trance state, light meditation or light hypnosis. The most usual way that the second triad of memory is accessed is through dreams.

DNA activation truly begins at its first level, if you will, in order for third triad thinking. It is a simple change in brain patterning and although much more rare, it is still seen by most other higher dimensional beings as 'normal' within a third and indeed a fourth dimensional thinking individual.

DNA activation, once started, begins to trigger more and more memories. These memories then go 'outside' of that third triad, if you will, and then become what we call 'celestial' memory.

This is memory not just from those individuals who are living or who have lived upon your planet Earth, but from individuals who are living or who have lived upon other planetary systems. Yet these individuals who have lived before are indeed you, for it is within this celestial memory that you remember your own 'past lives' if you will.

Still seen in a linear sense, even though this is now what we would call a 'fifth dimensional awareness'.

In truth, accessing the memories of other beings from other planetary systems and accessing your own 'past life' memories are one and the same thing from our perspective.

Celestial Memories

So the individual who 'remembers' living on the planet Sirius, or who recognised her face when looking in the mirror as a Pleiadian face, or who dreams of a beautiful crystal city that they know is upon the planet Lyra - all these are what we would call 'celestial memories'.

It is the celestial memories that 'came online' for you (for those we call 'starseeds') in your month of October in your year of 2016.

More and more starseeds are now being flooded with these 'memories'.

As you read these words, the 'keys, codes and triggers' to these memories are here in written form on the page before you. For it is our role as guides and 'assistants of light' to trigger you into these memories.

These 'memories' include not just memory of experience or richness of knowledge, but include blueprints for free energy, transportation, organic technology, healing and many other things you may perceive as wondrous and the stuff that miracles are made of.

Yet all these blueprints are your birthright. For you as human beings are here to undergo this process that we call 'ascension', and this is the reason you are here incarnated now upon your planet Earth.

This celestial memory is also that which we call 'the twelve strand DNA star crystalline matrix' or the 'twelfth dimensional gateway'.

It is a 'seed point', called such because the energetic frequency of ascension expands from this point.

The memories of all your incarnations are available at this point. Every incarnation you have held within a linear sense from the moment of your inception, be it on a planet related to Sirius, Pleiades or Lyra or any other inception point planet.

Most starseeds on Earth today hold inception points within these three planetary systems, Sirius, Pleiades and Lyra. There are those who hold Andromedan and Arcturian inception points on an individualised level (although these points are often inception points for the group soul). Within the Andromeda galaxy are a vast number of planetary systems and stars that are not named yet by your planet, or are even in awareness within your consciousness (except as a knowing of the vastness of the universe/multiverse within the starseed's fields).

The First Triad of Higher Memory

We could call this celestial memory (or twelfth dimensional gateway) 'the first triad' of 'higher memory'.

Therefore we can visualise six triads in this particular model.

Three 'linear memory templates'.

And three higher, non-linear memory templates (even though you may remember these experiences in a linear order, this is so your third dimensional brain can make sense of the experience even though these are non-linear experiences and thus non-linear memories).

So if we imagine that the DNA (the double helix) moves into a different formation and twelve strands of that DNA group together, this formation or activation will enable you to access all the memories of all your incarnations.

We could also say that the *memories themselves* are what triggers the twelve strand DNA formation! In truth, this is simultaneous (the memories and the DNA formation occur simultaneously).

The Chicken or the Egg?

This is often a difficult concept to process. Perhaps to assist you in opening your mind into this kind of expansion, one could ask the age-old question: What came first, the chicken or the egg?

Only those thinking in a linear sense will debate this question and try as they might, they cannot come up with an answer that makes any real sense to them simply because the answer is non-linear.

The answer to this age-old conundrum is *both*. The chicken and the egg were formulated together, simultaneously at the same time as DNA sought to express itself in all forms. It is exactly the same with your memories and the DNA formation. One does not create the other. They are both triggered simultaneously, together, at the same time.

The main purpose for this transmission is to look at the celestial memory level, the first triad of 'higher memory', and how you may be experiencing this at this time or to offer the keys, codes and triggers to assist you with this memory template.

This includes the twin flame experience and the full anchoring of the vertical axis as you begin to become familiar with the dodecahedron matrix formation that is the true expression of all that you are.

Yet we can go further and draw your attention to the fact that we can give name to the second and the third triads of higher memory, and give explanations as to what these signify.

Whilst it is the celestial level first triad of higher memory that the starseeds are currently experiencing at time of transmission (2017), there are a smaller group of starseeds experiencing memories and the perspectives of the second and third triads of higher memory.

These memories will come in flashes and glimpses and processing of these will be very unique. The channels amongst you and those in conscious 'contact' with the extraterrestrial, angelic realms and quantum fields will almost assuredly be experiencing memories from these triads as the 'extraterrestrials, angels and beings within the quantum fields' ARE the triads themselves!

For 'memory', just like 'thought', is a living consciousness. The triads are dimensions and every 'being' from that dimension is an expression of that dimension.

Oversoul

We could indeed say that each dimension is an 'oversoul' for the individual that resides within that dimension.

The same could be said for a planet, sun, moon or entire galaxy. Indeed *you* are aspects of the oversoul or Logos (or galactic triad) for your entire galaxy. Each aspect is a fragment or piece of the original creator aspect, yet each fragment or piece is created as an absolute replica of that original creator aspect. Each creator aspect is a holographic replica of the higher creator aspect, so on and so forth until Source and 'back out the other side' if you will, into a reverse fractal. Each hologram an infinite movement.

It is not conceivable to 'see' the whole picture of reality here. Even 'we', the White Winged Collective Consciousness of Nine, do not see the whole picture of reality or hold the concept within the understanding of our fields in its completeness. *Yet it can be felt* not only by us, but by *you*.

You can *feel* this larger picture that we speak of, and you do this not by going outwards and outwards into the fractality of the macrocosm, but by going inwards into the holographic nature of the microcosm and the zero point.

You shall find this that we speak of within the heart. This is where the knowledge lies through feeling, for the heart is *the seat of God* and when you combine this with the power of the solar plexus and look through the cosmic quantum window that is the pineal gland/third eye/brow chakra and activate the other energy centre/chakra points, you will be able to translate the meaning of this higher memory and transform all that you are. This is the ascension process.

The first triad of higher memory, we can call the twelve strand star crystalline matrix (or celestial matrix). For indeed it is an infinite matrix of expression.

The second triad of higher memory, we would refer to as the quantum sun crystalline matrix (or solar matrix). This is the memory field for the group soul. You are, each of you, part of a group soul and when you awaken group soul memory, you would be activating a higher DNA strand formation and thinking from the solar matrix perspective.

The reason why we would refer to this as a 'quantum sun' is that the DNA has moved into a quantum non-linear expression at this point and the 'sun' we refer to here is the Central Sun/galactic core. We are looking at a 144 DNA strand formation here.

The third triad of higher memory is that which we would call the diamond matrix (or Source field matrix). This is the perspective of Source, and the holding of the memories of Source and every creation and incarnation, including the memories of spiralling down from non-physical thought into a distortion of non-physical thought and into matter. The memories from this vantage point are so very personal and will be unique to each individual. Yet one individual can explain the memories of this triad and another can resonate with the knowing of that same memory.

The Nine Triads of the Matrix

In order to look at the full matrix construction, we would present the nine triad model. The nine triads of the matrix.

Indeed we can say to you that this is what 'we', the 'White Winged Collective Consciousness of Nine', are. We are the nine triads of the matrix of which we speak. Each of you have this formation of 'nine' and each of you can communicate with this formation of nine as our conduit communicates with us.

In this model, the first triad we speak of is actually *three triads*.

The second triad is three more triads.

The third triad is three more triads.

So we have the 'nine triads of the matrix'.

Explaining the Nine Triads

First three triads of the matrix (also known as the 'twelfth dimensional gateway'). The activation of the celestial self or celestial memory.

Within these three triads, we would have three 'aspects' if you will, relating to the dimensions and densities of reality.

Each of these triads are *living entities*, living conscious structures, known by many names and they present to you in many forms.

We would need to go into advanced mathematics and physics here to explain what these are. Our conduit does not have the conceptual terminology for us to present full explanation here. Know, to the biologists amongst you, we are speaking here of 'quantum resonance' within DNA fields (that which you would know as 'junk DNA'). We could refer to the activation of these DNA strands as 'biological transmutation'.

We could liken this first triad on a biological level to the chemicals within your known DNA sequence: adenine, guanine, cytosine, and thymine.

We list here the four you are aware of, yet within the model we use there will be twelve of these chemicals. Each one linking to 'one strand' if you will, of the DNA structure.

When moving beyond the twelve strand into the 144 strand DNA, then each of these chemicals 'replicate' themselves, if you will, creating quantum versions of themselves.

This process creates a 'grid of light'. For each of the DNA chemicals, when activated, move into a 'Flower of Life' pattern within the DNA and begin to spin. They also begin to radiate (and move into what we could call a 'radio frequency waveband'). They are then able to communicate with each other.

The Gaia Grid

What this means for the starseeds is a telepathic grid created between them. Yet this also links telepathically to the grids of the Earth, the 'Gaia grid', and to the grids within the universe and cosmos, the 'galactic grid'.

Once your awareness moves into the galactic grid (or creates the galactic grid, harmonises with it, merges with it... all the same process), you will have fully activated these nine triads of the matrix.

What makes this so interesting for you starseeds on Earth at this point is that you do not have to 'wait' one hundred years for this to occur!

It is true that this is a process and that there will be many stages to go through, many stargates to pass through, if you will.

One hundred years from where you are in your current time period will look very different to how your planet looks today. In fact, if a time traveller from one hundred years into the future were to visit you now in your current time period, they would indeed act, think and look 'extraterrestrial' to you (just as you may look to your ancestors of one hundred years past). Yet your future selves, or descendants (same thing), will be fully realised 'fourth density humans'.

We realise that these concepts are difficult for many of you to grasp. It is the scientists amongst you, within the field of 'fringe science' or 'cutting edge physics', that present this information to you in the more technical form.

It is just as much of a challenge for our conduit, Magenta Pixie, to grasp these concepts as it is for you, the reader of our words.

Yet our conduit delivers the same information as the 'new physicists' of which we speak, yet in a different form. It is the activation we present to you, through her, via language of light interpretation that we call 'the dream' or 'the story'.

Therefore it matters not if you do not consciously understand and process the model of DNA activation and higher memory that we present here. As you go forward, you will begin to understand more and more.

What is most important is that you make your own personal connection with your higher guidance system, the crystalline matrix, and change your brainwave patterning. You then begin to tune your radio frequencies to a different dial and thus access memory at a celestial, solar and galactic level.

This is what we are here to assist you with, within this transmission. Our previous transmission was the information regarding your own personal matrix and mastery over it, so you may become sovereign and immune from matrix hijacking.

This transmission takes the sovereignty to the next level, that of designing your matrix in the first place!

Architect of the Matrix

You are the architect of your own matrix and when you stand as the architect, then only you know the patterns needed to construct the structure! The plans and patterns are hidden in the safe vault within the inner recesses of the memory mind surrounded by 'angelic guards' that are from your true higher planetary lineage. They cannot be accessed by anyone but yourself.

They are hermetically sealed within a 'Christ consciousness vault', sealed with the power and the truth of the 144,000 on Earth. Only you can access them.

Those who would hijack the matrix of others have looked extensively for the plans, patterns and blueprints that would enable you to construct your matrix.

Due to the fact that the plans and blueprints are hermetically sealed within the Christ consciousness safe vault, they have been unable to access the blueprints.

Whilst they have been able to create false chambers, false guards and new landscapes, hiding the Christ consciousness vaults from your view, they have never been able to access them. It is *not possible* for another being to access the blueprint of another being in the fullest sense of the meaning. Other beings can falsely lead you into a situation whereby you 'hijack yourself' if you will, but you cannot be fully hijacked by another. The material in our previous transmission *Masters of the Matrix* presents the formula for sovereignty and the 'immunity from hijacking and infiltration' which goes with it. Liberty and self- actualisation (and therefore the pathways to true ascension are cleared).

Therefore whilst hijacking codes, misleading, falsely guiding and replacing truth with falsehood have been strategies employed, the actual matrix blueprints at their very core have always been and shall always remain inaccessible.

These individuals, those of the service-to-self structure, the 'hijackers' shall we call them?... these hijackers could not find the pure golden and extremely valuable blueprints they so desperately coveted. In their anger at being thwarted this way by creation itself, they employed a different

119

tactic. That which perhaps you may know as 'the dog in the manger'.

They decided that if they could not access the golden blueprints to the matrix systems, then neither would you. They therefore misled you and confused you, so much that you lost your bearings. You were a ship afloat without a compass, if you will. You 'forgot' the way to the Christ consciousness safe vault and you could not access your own golden blueprints!

Therefore you did not know how to construct your matrix, and thus reality. What we are saying here is that *they took away your memories*.

On the one hand, this was decided by the unified aspect of you who split itself into two parts: the service-to-self polarised aspect and the service-to-others polarised aspect in order to 'play a game' if you will, and experience itself.

It is important for you to hold this higher galactic perspective in order to understand the game and see the bigger picture. This prevents you from moving into the victim/saviour mentality.

Yet within the polarised perspectives, it is important for you to now understand what occurred and how as an aspect of yourself was not 'lost' by accident, it was hidden from you because those that wanted it *could not have it*.

Now, upon your Earth, it is time for you to find this lost aspect of self. It is time for you to remember the way back to the Christ consciousness safe vault, merge as one with the hermetic seal and open the blueprint or plan. Once you have memorised the blueprint, you stand as the architect and are able to build your matrix.

The Story

Do you understand here what the dream is? What the story is? For whilst we can speak of colour rays, spiritual levels, esoteric terms and biological structures, it is the dream or story that holds the activation.

There are many stories, and the story we would draw your attention to at this time is the story of *the lost city of Atlantis*.

One does not need to be a master in cellular biology or quantum physics in order to find the blueprint. One simply needs to experience the story.

We also provide a guided meditation in order for you to do just that, experience the story and find the hermetically sealed vault that contains the golden blueprints to *your* matrix field.

The Great Reveal

But firstly, we give you a little more background information in order to take our place in the 'great reveal' and deliver to you yet more activation codes.

So the question you may ask at this juncture is, "What does all this have to do with the lost city of Atlantis?"

Remember we said you had lost something? *Or more to the point, that something had been taken from you?* Well, the codes lie in the Atlantean memories that you all hold.

The golden blueprints to the matrix are your Atlantean memories and as we have said, you did not lose these memories, *they were hidden from you.*

Therefore we could quite truthfully say that Atlantis is not the lost city... it is the *hidden city.*

Within this 'great reveal' occurring on your planet right now is the finding of the hidden city of Atlantis.

Together, we the White Winged Collective Consciousness of Nine, through our conduit Magenta Pixie, are going to find the hidden city of Atlantis.

8

Hidden City of Atlantis

So what is it that you have 'lost'? Or rather, what is it that has been taken and is hidden?

These are the original DNA code formations that we refer to as 'the infinite helix', the 'twelve strand formation', the 'blueprints/templates for the 144,000 warriors of light' or 'sealed servants'.

These were 'lost','stolen' or 'deactivated' depending on perspective. This final deactivation occurred with what is known as 'the fall of Atlantis'.

We would take you back to Atlantean times. This is a period of prehistory (prior to your known history) on your planet Earth. This is a time period where magick still existed, but not in the form that we have already discussed, that which we may call within the elemental kingdom or original Middle World.

The Atlantean times came later than this period in a linear sense, and we can truthfully say that Atlantis was not a 'place' but a time period. Your entire planet was what you would know as 'Atlantis'.

Beyond the Triple Helix

After the original Middle World, and prior to Atlantis, was the time period known as Lemuria (Mu). The story of Lemuria and Atlantis are a whole other transmission!

However, we will say what needs to be said regarding Atlantis in relation to the lost codes within the DNA, that you are now reconstructing in their new formation and moving back into the regrouping of the twelve strands. Moving from the carbon-based double helix formation into the triple helix crystalline formation, and beyond the triple helix into what we may call the 'infinite helix'.

The Atlanteans, after many years became master geneticists and masters of technology. They were keepers of the powerful crystals and crystal generators and they learned to access crystal technology, giving them many powers and skills.

We speak metaphorically and in code here due to this story being an ongoing one, and in order to keep the hermetical sealing in place until such time it can be opened on a global scale. Suffice it to say, that many of these Atlantean masters moved into what we would call 'the god complex' and created for themselves the reality whereby not only did they experience their own downfall but also the downfall of all humanity.

Yet there were some we may refer to as the Atlantean priests (many of these individuals are known in your current time period as activated starseeds who teach the way), who learned how to 'bend time' if you will. For there were many experiments being conducted, at the time, into the very fabric of reality.

The Golden Triad of Ascension Grid

The Atlanteans, along with their ability to bend time, also learned how to 'preserve information and codes within crystals and crystalline matter'.

So we say to you, look to all crystals and all that you consider crystalline. When you place these elements together, you create a crystal grid or network and this network is the activator for the reconstruction of the DNA fields and ultimately full memory recall of the entire story.

Those who read or listen to this transmission instantly become part of a crystalline energetic grid or network. We may call this network the 'golden triad of ascension grid', a telepathic union created by those who connect with this work/transmission and the material herein.

All those who draw down these transmissions, as pure connected conduits of light, are able to present the information within the incoming download or monad as a grid of this type.

Why do we refer to this grid?

This grid we speak of, the golden triad of ascension grid, and other grids like it, are grids of consciousness. We may also say 'grids of crystalline consciousness'. These ARE the very same grids that are 'crystalline matter' that were utilised for preservation of the information and codes we speak of, those that were consciously created by the Atlantean priests. Their 'bending of time' was the conscious transference of information through these networks and grids, to be activated on or around the 2012 time period (with manifestation and processing set to occur between 2017 and 2021).

There are a great many grids of this type in circulation across your planet at this time. The golden triad of ascension is only one.

We speak in veiled terms here for good reason. We do you a disservice if we do not. We give explanation as much as we are able, whilst still preserving the mystery of this situation. The mystery is all part of the code itself, so it must be preserved along with the respect and acknowledgement of your free will.

We provide many keys and codes regarding the unlocking of these mysteries and metaphors, and the language of light is utilised muchly so that your DNA matrix fields are communicated with directly.

This is the legacy left for you from the Atlantean priests, your past selves, those who learned to bend time by preserving knowledge within crystalline matter.

There is much to be learned from the Atlantean civilisation. You see here examples of what NOT to do, for in many ways you do NOT wish to 'repeat history' as it were. Yet also there is much richness to be gained and information to decode, from those past aspects of yourselves as the Atlantean priests of good intent and service-to-others polarisation.

If one were to think of this 'Atlantean consciousness' as a place, one can create this place within one's fifth dimensional imagination fields of hyperspace. The name we give to this place holds memory triggers within the sounds of the place title and within the visualised images of light that it conjures up in your mind. We call this place the 'Emerald City of Krysta.'

This 'place' is known to you, within your DNA memory fields specific to the Atlantean codes.

All one needs to say is, "I wish to remember the Emerald City of Krysta." This will create 'emerald Kristos sphere templates' within the DNA memory codons which create a fractalised geometric lattice. This is a major building block into the crystalline structure and thus the 'rainbow body of light'.

The hidden city of Atlantis is yours to find and we provide, through this transmission and the resulting golden triad of ascension grid, the tools, keys, codes and triggers with which to find it.

9

Mer-Ka-Bah Magick and Emotional Alchemy

We have spoken of the vertical pillar of light, and the pivot point that is Middle World.

The Middle World before known history, before the fall down the frequencies, the descension from the crystalline matrix into the double helix DNA formation.

Middle World as it was in the past and Middle World as it shall be in the future (albeit in a different form as you have jumped timelines, if you will) is the same place.

The future and the past are one and are created from the central vantage point, the zero point that is the pivot point. You control the pivot point, therefore you control the structure of reality.

One can access the control of this structure and the creation of one's reality by standing within awareness of the matrix grid field. The template for the individualised soul.

We would take you through a visualisation of the matrix structure and simultaneously provide the keys, codes and triggers for the memory of this structure. This is the structure that is you, your planet, your galaxy, your universe, your sun and reality and thought itself.

Yet we start with the knowing that this structure is you, for you are all things. Your awareness of the matrix structure will instantly trigger your full knowing of your superimposed and merged unity with all things and with all realities.

We have spoken of the vertical pillar of light.

We have shown you the pillar of light as it moves upwards above you into the cosmic reality and that of the overworld.

We have shown you the pillar of light as it moves downwards into the dark forest, the magickal place of manifestation and that of the underworld.

Above you, somewhere within that stream of light is the twin flame aspect, your true twin flame, standing as the aspect of self that calls the vibrational match for the partner of destiny into your reality. Shining as a calling to the node points within your blueprint, the convergence of timelines within the geometry of your creation.

We know that the upward moving aspect of the vertical pillar of light and the downward moving aspect of the vertical pillar of light connect within the same place.

If you keep moving upward, you will come back to self at the pivot point. If you keep moving downwards, you will come back to self at the pivot point.

Emotional Alchemy

The awareness of this is the pole shift, the knowing that the crown is the base/root and the root/base is the crown. For if you anchor yourself within the pivot point, you can twist and spin and spiral the structure around yourself as a Whirling Dervish of creation within the creational wheel of living geometry. All one has to do is see the thought. The visualisation. The story. Thus leading to the emotional reaction within alignment to the geometric formation. The visualisation of the vision, the story, the memory and the combined emotion leads to emotional alchemy.

That which alchemises one form into a higher form of itself by taking two elements and merging them together.

You stand at the point of Middle World which is the expression of your physical reality. Middle World will be a direct representation of your state of consciousness and the dimension in which you reside (the dimensional construct of mind that you think with), and thus will be a direct representation of your DNA structure. Hence the elemental and magickal beings that existed in Middle World's 'past' and that exist (in potential) in Middle World's future.

So you, the you that you are and that you experience, stands within the central point of the vertical pillar of light. You look upwards to the cosmic/overworld aspect. You look downwards to the Earth/underworld aspect. You are aware of above and below and of up and down.

Now you look straight in front of you. Once you have full awareness of the vertical pillar of light and that you stand at the central point of the vertical pillar of light, there is nothing but a void in front of you. Blackness, the blackness of the universal fabric or the night sky. Or you may see pure white light or a colourless 'nothingness'. However you visualise this, when first constructing the geometry and standing as the architect, you see the vertical pillar of light as your first aspect to the construction.

We understand that the guided visualisation will assist you here and indeed we provide this within this transmission. Yet so too do we unravel the construction for you, for those who wish to truly know, to truly feel, to truly unify with the individualised matrix that is the true you and will always be the true you. For there is no beginning and no end to the matrix. The matrix is the Alpha and the Omega, the first and the last, the birth and the death, the start point and the end point. The matrix stands as these aspects simultaneously and whilst we understand the challenge of assimilating this unified geometry into a linear understanding, *indeed you can do this*.

For you are 'the warrior' and you are 'the wizard' and you are 'the wanderer' and you are 'the way'. When you know the way and can access the way, you can show the way and you shall then stand as the 'wayshower' and this is your purpose. *For as you learn, so you do teach and as you follow, so you do lead.*

You stand as the central point within the vertical axis of the matrix, that which we call 'the vertical pillar of light' and you look forward in front of you into the void of space and time.

The Horizontal Rainbow Bridge Pathway

Then you begin to fill the void with your visualisation. As you look in front of you, you see a brightly coloured rainbow that stretches out before you in an infinite stream of forward moving momentum. Like a ribbon in space, setting a pathway before you that you can walk and follow should you so choose. You see that this rainbow ribbon branches off into many streams, potential forks in the road, layer upon layer in infinite measure. This is that which we call the 'horizontal rainbow bridge pathway' and it signifies the future.

The ribbons that branch off into the void in infinite form are the potentials within the future. One ribbon for every thought you have and every choice you make and every action you take. So above you, you have the white light of the vertical pillar of light. Below you, you have the white light of the vertical pillar of light. And in front of you, stretching into infinity, you have the horizontal rainbow bridge pathway.

You have up. You have down. You have forward.

The higher dimensions/heaven realms/cosmic reality/overworld.

The lower dimensions/hell realms/Earth reality/underworld.

The rainbow bridge that connects worlds to worlds and spirals to spirals. The living fabric of the matrix that responds to the electrical charge within your DNA fields that is intentionalised and directed through your higher thought and your alchemised emotions.

The Sacred Cross of Creation

We remind you again that this up/down does not mean good or bad. We use the terms 'heaven' and 'hell' to trigger your own knowing into the truth of the geometric reality that is beautiful and vast and intelligent and is love. This has been distorted for you into 'above is light and good' and 'below is dark and evil'. This distorts your reality so that you may not embrace the sacred cross of creation.

Remember we told you of the 'dog in the manger'? That those we call the 'hijackers' could not access the blueprints? Therefore they distorted the reality construct so that you could not find them yourselves. What are these blueprints? They are your individualised matrix! They are you!

How can you ascend and transform if you cannot find yourself?

They could not find these blueprints but they did not want you to find them either. So reality was distorted and remains distorted.

You are only to look up and not to look down. Yet you can only look up, and see up as so far out of your reach. You are far too afraid to look down, so you pretend down does not exist. Yet up is you and down is you, the true you. This truth has been hidden from you so that you could not find the blueprints to creation and thus freedom.

Yet the hijackers underestimated the power of light, love and truth and the crystalline and diamond potentials within the starseed beings. They underestimated the abilities of the starseeds to remember, to teach in oh-so-many varied ways, to learn, to understand, to expand and to share, share, share!

Remember, it matters not if you are not in full processing and understanding of the explanations we deliver here. We present to our conduit an energetic stream of reality for her to interpret. For words are not the teaching, it is energy that is the teaching. Words are simply the activation and we give you the activations now.

So we say to you, look down with as much wonder as you look up. All is the same place, the same space, the same aspect. When you access the sacred cross of creation you will know that you will find self and Source *in any direction you take.*

So you look up and you see above, the pillar of light that is the vertical axis. You look down and see below, the pillar of light that is the vertical axis. You look forward, in front of you, and see the rainbow ribbon that is the horizontal rainbow bridge pathway.

Now we want you to look behind you...

Within the void, you will see the other part of the horizontal rainbow bridge pathway stretching behind you into infinity, with streams and ribbons branching off, fading into invisibility as the potentials and choices and actions you did not take.

Now you look in front of you and see your future and all that you can be. Now you look behind you and see your past and all that you once were.

Now you look above you and see all that you can be. Now you look below you and see all that you once were.

Up and down, forward and back. They are all the same.

Now you stand within the zero point aspect of the sacred cross of creation, and now you may know why you stand on a pivot point *for you can change these aspects at will simply by the virtue of your own thought.*

You can swivel the entire cross so that up becomes forward, forward becomes down, and down becomes behind.

One more shift and up becomes down, forward becomes behind, and so on.

So what exactly is this knowledge useful for? How is the visualisation of the movement helpful to you?

This is all to do with memory. You are blueprinted or 'programmed' if you will, to remember who you are and what you are here to do. This knowledge is a trigger into those memories. It is a reminder of that which you already know. Visualisation of the movement will activate the DNA and trigger the memory. This begins a journey of transformation, transmutation and upgrade.

Why are we presenting this teaching?

We present this teaching as the contract between us, the White Winged Collective Consciousness of Nine, and our conduit Magenta Pixie was to do this work and to present the teaching in this way. The contract was made in order to trigger Magenta's own memory and awakening, and for her to assist in triggering the awakening of others simultaneously so you may all awaken and learn alongside one another, as a team, as a family of light.

Mer-Ka-Bah Magick!

It may seem to some of you that this is but a child's game. It may seem to some of you that this is frivolous and meaningless. Yet to some of you, indeed many of you, you instantly recognise the geometry of which we speak.

You are fully aware that this is the inner you, the true you, and that the processing of this Flower of Life patterning all around you has been calling you.

You are aware of yourself as a sacred geometric intelligent structure beyond the physical body that you inhabit.

The teaching we present here, the construction of the matrix and how to stand as the Architect of the Matrix, is deep, connected work with your light body. The rainbow body aspect of self. It is profound work with your Mer-Ka-Bah. Indeed it is *Mer-Ka-Bah magick!!*

In order to understand the Matrix Architecture and Mer-Ka-Bah magick, you need to be familiar with emotional alchemy.

In our transmission *Masters of the Matrix* we spoke of emotional integration and how to integrate every emotion so that integration of the emotion is the code that sets within the matrix computer rather than the emotion itself. This is what many of you know as 'shadow work'. This emotional integration, unravelling and, ultimately, healing of trauma is a necessary part of ascension.

In this transmission, we take the emotional integration one step further and we present to you 'emotional alchemy'.

A most aligned way to understand emotional alchemy is to look at the service-to-others and the service-to-self vibrations.

This, for many, can be a battle mentality. Alternatively, there are others who 'turn a blind eye' as it were, to the atrocities that the service-to-self groups have committed and move into a transcendent state within their lives, a state that says, "I will ignore you and if I ignore you, then you do not exist. I will do this by continually reminding myself that everything is perfect and wonderful and all is as it should be."

The individual in the transcendent state moves their focus into the truths of the higher dimensions without integrating the third dimensional truth. This is known as 'skimming above' or 'bypassing'.

Both these presentations are unhealthy for the bodymind. They are unhealthy for the matrix codes are received as 'ignoring' or 'burying' or creating for oneself a 'false light'. This code then sets within the matrix and the responding vibrational structure is created within the individual's third dimensional life.

This can create disharmonies within the spiritual, psychological, emotional and physical aspects of the bodymind.

Therefore how does one move away from battle mentality, skipping over or bypassing?

Forgiveness of the opposing aspect is a most aligned emotion to utilise. When one uses forgiveness, then it is the emotion of forgiveness and its related emotion - compassion - that sets as the code within the matrix. Alchemising these emotions together is the other aspect to Mer-Ka-Bah magick.

Matrix Architecture + Emotional Alchemy = Mer-Ka-Bah Magick

This 'mathematical equation' is a DNA trigger to the keys and codes of cellular memory/original Source memory and thus the knowledge of *who you are.*

Let us look at this again.

Matrix Architecture + Emotional Alchemy = Mer-Ka-Bah Magick

Loving the Opposing Polarity

How do we forgive the service-to-self structures for the atrocities and crimes against humanity that they have committed? In fact, how can we possibly love them when we look at the things they have done?

We have spoken before of a circle around you. This circle is the outside reflection of self and contains within it all that is 'other'.

In the truest reality, there is no 'other'. All are simply illusionary representations, aspects or reflections of self.

Some of these illusionary representations are reflections of your light and others are your shadow.

Within the light, there are degrees of brilliance and illumination, and within the shadows are the varying shades of grey into darkness.

Yet all stand within the circle as 'other' and so too as 'self'.

If one aspect is seen with anger, then so too is the anger directed inward as well as outward. Therefore love of other is also self-love.

Self-love is the key to enlightenment and ascension, therefore self-love must be love of other.

There is a journey to be undertaken here, the energetic fields of higher intelligence around you hold no expectations of how quickly you must perform this act of self-love (and thus love of other). In fact, there is no expectation of you on any level for the energetic fields of higher intelligence are also other and thus self.

It is easy for most of you to love the reflections of your light, yet it is not so easy to love the reflections of your shadow. Yet this is the requirement for enlightenment and fully realised ascension (there can still be ascension within confusion when the heart is open, yet fully realised ascension is the teaching we present here).

Forgiveness is a tool to lead you into that love we speak of, and the kind of love you are looking for is unconditional love.

Yet how can you forgive those who have trespassed against you, you ask?

This is a journey and is rarely instantaneous, except for the purist and most innocent amongst you (most often the infant newly incarnated).

The journey involves the integration of self. When the emotions are integrated and move into balance, then forgiveness and unconditional love is much easier. We spoke of emotional integration in our previous transmission *Masters of the Matrix* but let us recap in summary...

Acknowledgement

Gratitude

Analysis

Integration

When we speak of forgiveness, it does not mean no longer acknowledging the misdeeds of another. One stands strong for justice upon the physical level of third dimensional incarnation, but one stands strong for justice *with fairness.*

Forgiveness is simply another facet of love, another energy that is part of unconditional love.

Compassion is the key here. When compassion is merged with forgiveness, then this translates and transmutes to unconditional love.

This is *emotional alchemy.*

Two original 'base metal' emotions, merged together to transform or 'alchemise' into a higher emotion. Although in truth, compassion and forgiveness are already 'golden emotions' if you will.

Compassion + Forgiveness = Unconditional Love

We now have two mathematical equations for you to process. We use here the language of light, blending the letter with the number to create the 'alphabetical numeral'.

Your DNA fields respond to number and mathematical equation *for this is what you are.*

Do not be concerned if you are not processing this instantly. This is not to be expected and the processing (whilst helpful and activating in and of itself) is not needed for the ascension process and the journey into enlightenment and self-actualisation.

Let us look again at these mathematical language of light equations...

Matrix Architecture + Emotional Alchemy = Mer-Ka-Bah Magick

Compassion + Forgiveness = Unconditional Love

We can also include another most triggering equation here...

Lovelight + Lightlove = Bliss Charged Love

We have here a 'golden triad' of ascension equations as DNA activating memory triggers.

Philosopher's Stone

All emotions can be merged together to create a 'higher version' of the original emotions. The 'turning lead into gold' metaphor stands true for the emotions you experience as third density physically incarnated humans.

The 'philosopher's stone' here is your own emotional intelligence or emotional focus as you transmute lower emotions into higher ones. As you do this, you finally move into the emotion of 'bliss' which carries the frequency of the golden mean. This emotion is the key to change the cellular structure of your physical form, creating the 'light body'.

Emotional alchemy, therefore, is the key to light body transformation (and this is ascension and total recall of soul memory).

Once you have moved through emotional integration and emotional alchemy, you have 'higher tools' at your disposal, if you will, regarding loving your shadow (the service-to-self structures).

Once you are aware that ALL other structures are presentations of self and that *there is no other* then it is much easier to understand self-love and the love of other.

The Circle of Love

Therefore you can envisage a circle around you. You are in the centre of this circle and all 'other' structures (on your planet and beyond) surround you.

You can visualise this as being 'you' in the middle of the circle surrounded by 'everyone else'.

Or you can visualise the 'central point of you' (your heart, for this exercise is that of unconditional love) surrounded by all other aspects of you (including the shadow). Both visualisations create the same energetic that you are looking for, that of completeness and integration.

If within the structures surrounding you, there is *just one* person, structure or aspect that you do not like or hate or feel any other negative emotion towards then *you break the circle.*

But as we have said, this is a journey and one cannot click their fingers and forgive those who have trespassed against them in one swift moment. The emotional integration work followed by the emotional alchemy is a most aligned process in order to be able to complete the circle.

The golden triad of ascension equations are keys into this understanding...

Matrix Architecture + Emotional Alchemy = Mer-Ka-Bah Magick

Compassion + Forgiveness = Unconditional Love

Lovelight + Lightlove = Bliss Charged Love

It matters not how much time this takes. There is no hurry, no rush and no deadline.

It is important to remember that when it comes to forgiveness of the opposing polarity, e.g. an Illuminati/cabal/elite group that has enslaved you and your family, *one does not have to forgive the behaviour.*

Boundaries, Borders and Walls

One stands strong within the third dimensional physical field and takes a stand within the integrity, justice, honour and warrior template. Thus creating the solar plexus strength of *boundaries and borders* that cannot and will not be crossed. An aspect of your sovereignty is the boundaries and borders you create.

You then step into the 'indigo uprising' or the 'starseed revolution' frequency, which is a merge of the balanced and strong third dimensional perspective and the higher multidimensional perspective.

One then moves into forgiveness of the soul or soul family/soul group, rather than the behaviour the soul has displayed. This is much easier to do for those who have been trespassed against.

Eventually, as you progress higher in your expansion and integration, you will be able to personify *the behaviour itself* and allow that behaviour personification to take its place within the circle of love. You then see *the soul of the behaviour* as if it were a person or construct, and you work within the realms of forgiveness/compassion and unconditional love *for that behaviour* yet you *never* lose sight of the boundaries, borders and walls that stand as tools for your sovereignty.

You take your part within the 'indigo uprising' as well as being a fully alchemised being, glowing with golden light, vibrating and indeed radiating with the golden tone of the universe, alight with the brilliance of unconditional love.

10

The Fall

How did this fall occur?

We will explain this by responding to one of the questions you have asked us...

I am currently reading 'The Book of Enoch*, and how it describes the 'fall' of certain angels. Azazyel is mentioned as one of the leaders. May I ask you, Magenta Pixie/the Nine, how did the consciousness of the aforementioned angel perceive the humans, which he\she\it started to covet and desired to merge with and produce children? Simply, at that time, what was the state of the consciousness of the angel? Curiosity? Driven by loneliness that projected a desire for control? There is no judgement here, from my point of view, simply an honest attempt to gauge the state of being which initiated the 'fall'.

This is a question of a very high frequency. The seeker in his/her quest for the knowledge of reality asks many questions and each question is a match to the vibrational state of the seeker.

We would firstly respond by replying that there are two potential 'answers' here from two different perspectives.

We have spoken before of how all is metaphor, and within these ancient texts there is much truth yet much is metaphor. Yet the metaphors for energies and frequencies hold a vibrational match within the physical dimension and in many cases these can be literal presentations of the story.

Indeed the literal presentations of people, situations and events are preserved and passed down as factual story. Some retain much of the

---

* *The Book of Enoch* (also known as *1 Enoch*) is an ancient apocryphal religious text. It is ascribed to Enoch, an Old Testament character who did not die like a normal human. The Bible states: "Enoch lived 365 years, walking in close fellowship with God. Then one day he disappeared, because God took him." In Kabbalistic traditions, Enoch was transformed into the archangel Metatron.

original source and others hold so much distortion as to be unrecognisable.

We shall therefore firstly respond to your question from the perspective of the metaphor. The story here is a trigger point (to your own unlocking of the inner DNA codons). A truthful tale of 'energy evolution' or indeed 'energy creation'.

We shall also respond from the original source vibrational match. The aligned reality to the metaphor of Azazyel.

1) The truthful energetic presentation. The 'match' to this metaphor (the non-physical/non-manifested/antimatter aspect). What the metaphor represents. Yet there are many metaphors (metaphors within metaphors), therefore we present the 'highest metaphor' that we can present given the terminology available to us through our conduit's fields.

2) The aligned physical representation of the metaphor. A story that is a metaphoric match to the truthful energetic presentation. This (as a manifested match to the formation of energy) will be actual, literal events that occurred on your planet on other quantum streams and timelines. These 'stories' have been accessed by the seers, dreamwalkers, clairvoyants and prophets on your planet and have been passed down just as if they were literal events within your current timeline. Some of these events were literal events within your current timeline, yet cannot be always perceived as such due to the fluctuation in quantum existences (a phenomena known to you as the 'Mandela effect'). So it is in alignment to say that these may or may not be actual, literal, real events that occurred on your planet, within your history and within your timeline.

Another way to explain these different perspectives is to say that there are different energetic matches to metaphors expressed differently within each dimension.

Suffice it to say, in many cases 'stories, tales and texts' can be absolute metaphor without any manifested match (either accurate, distorted or part-truth/part-distortion), an actual manifested match within an alternate timeline, or an actual manifested match within your current timeline.

The book of Enoch that you mention holds much truth and a great many keys, codes and triggers to your own activation and awakening the cellular memories within. This book that you speak of is a 'node point' in itself and presents in 'all timelines' (all timelines that are physical representations of third density, free will Earth undergoing ascension). There are many such texts of this kind, that stand as the node point, and more yet to be created in your future. For creation, specifically creation by starseeds stands strong within the probability fields of the Gaia matrix.

The story you speak of is a highly aligned metaphor for a truthful, non-physical presentation. This is a metaphor with a high degree of accuracy for the non-physical presentation. This is 'literal' only in the sense that there was (or is) a 'being', or more accurately a 'group matrix of individualised intelligence' that underwent (or is currently undergoing, depending on perspective) the 'fall' in frequency (or loss of code formation/memory).

Let us speak therefore of this group matrix as a single being by the name of Azazyel. This is not the 'original name' for this being, yet this name is a matching frequency. Therefore it matters not, for the energy of the name stands in alignment with the frequency or 'tone' of the soul matrix/being we speak of.

This being was (or is) what you would term 'extraterrestrial'.

One may or may not refer to this being as an 'angel' at this point, this would again depend on perspective.

From your perspective, this being was indeed 'an angel' for the positive polarisation was high. Yet this being was an entity that existed between the higher echelons of the fourth dimension and the lower echelons of the fifth, therefore there are perspectives whereby this being would *not* be referred to as an angel.

The story within this ancient text holds the higher metaphor as well as the historical source, therefore to refer to this being as an angel is most appropriate given the fact that the higher dimensional teachings and triggerings of the creational energy is held within this story.

This extraterrestrial fourth dimensional/lower fifth dimensional being was a 'master geneticist' if you will.

The desire to covet the Earth humans was based on the ability to produce a race, take part in the 'grand experiment' of Earth, seed aspects of Azazyel's race and store information upon Earth. This provided the situation where that stored information would evolve through a free will energetic. This was also very much about preservation of species, and creation of a new species.

This was personal to the being Azazyel, as this action contributed to Azazyel's individualisation as a soul matrix (in the context of this being's past).

The merging with and production of children was the seeding of a new genetic line. A creation of individuals, now known as 'humanity on Earth' from your perspective.

We have spoken before regarding the whys and wherefores of how the seeding occurred. Not through physical procreation but through the transfer of energies. (Physical procreation as genetic engineering occurred only when the soul/matrix in question incarnated into the physical beingness within matter.)

This action allowed the being Azazyel to move upwards in frequency and access the mid-levels of the fifth dimension.

However, Azazyel was not alone in the seeding of the human race on Earth. He was one being of many. We may call these the 'overseers of the experiment' if you will. We could also refer to these individuals collectively as 'the guardians' or 'the guardian race'. Many also would know these individuals as 'the ancient ones', 'the old ones', or the 'original souls'.

As we have previously said, the seeding of the human race originally was of pure service-to-others intent, yet this was infiltrated by service-to-self energetics.

Azazyel was of a partly service-to-others polarisation, or was on the path towards positive polarisation.

At that time, what was the state of the consciousness of the angel? Curiosity? Driven by loneliness that projected a desire for control?

The state of consciousness was that of 'wanting to achieve' or 'wanting to evolve'.

Azazyel understood the journey of the soul as an energy matrix and was motivated by the alignment to move upwards in frequency. The genetic manipulation was, from this being, perceived as an act of love and as an act of creation.

There were other beings within this group of extraterrestrials who were driven by a desire for control. Azazyel would not perceive itself (we say 'itself' for this being was neither male nor female as you would know it but of a 'third gender' shall we say?) as desiring control but desiring 'promotion' if you will. Promotion in the terms of achieving a higher status. Yet this being was not service-to-self for this being did not hold the belief system of "As long as I exist then it does not matter if others do not exist, for I am all there is."

This being 'loved' its creations and held genuine affection for the humans and was most invested in their journey. We cannot say this was in full service and surrender, therefore this being would be termed as partly polarised towards service-to-others.

Perhaps we can explain this in terms you will recognise by saying that this being 'made a mistake' or 'made a miscalculation'. This is not entirely accurate but we wish to clear up any confusion individuals may have about this being as a service-to-self or evil being. Indeed, this being did have an agenda to forward its own evolution and progression, yet simultaneously this being cared greatly for its creations just as a parent cares for its 'children'. This caring was expressed in a somewhat controlling way, yet the intention of this being was not to control but to evolve.

This being was not driven by loneliness for there was a great fullness of experience of 'other' in its life. Yet curiosity would indeed be an emotion that would fit, although this would be more akin to 'curiosity merged with excitement' regarding the outcome of Earth's human creations.

We shall now explain this story from the truthful energetic presentation, within the parameters of our conduit's fields.

Within this, we also respond to your original query about how the fall occurred.

As we have said, there are different perspectives expressed within each dimension.

Looking at the non-physical antimatter existence, we explain 'the fall', and with it the understanding of the matrix known as 'Azazyel' and similar individualised matrix structures.

We speak now from the highest truth we are able to access through our conduit's fields. All is, as we have said, metaphor. Yet there are levels (or dimensions) to metaphor.

Using the most aligned metaphor from 'Source perspective', presented within a linear pattern, our explanation is thus...

Source, the being with no name and all names found itself in a void. Source was as the void. A comfortable void of perfect expression of love and light simultaneously. There was no separation, no loneliness, no confusion. Just existence in a sea of unity. With no voice, no thought, no sound. Just forever in all things and forever in love.

Then, there came a moment upon the being with no name and all names. The thought is expressed as "I think, therefore I am." The thought was a vibration and was truth, intelligence and infinity. Yet the one thought, the one vibration, by its virtue of being separate from the oneness as a single thought/vibration, was a distortion. For all things expressed from Source as independent from Source is distortion from Source.

The vibration "I think, therefore I am" was the primordial sound of creation. It was the raw utterance of the maternal birthing of the first child, and therefore the geometry was forever changed.

"I think, therefore I am" as a vibration, stood strong. For indeed it was utmost truth. Yet for every action there is an equal and opposite reaction, so came the response to the first thought, the first vibration. The response of "Am I?"

This was the second distortion, yet still intelligent infinity was expressed. The vibration of "Am I?" was a further distortion for this was the expression of not-knowing from the all-knowing. This was the response to the primordial sound of creation. It was the raw utterance of the maternal birthing of the second child, therefore the geometry was forever changed.

In response to the distortions/vibrations, original Source did send forth a third distortion/vibration. This was the expression/desire/creation template of "I wish to experience all and everything." This, in response to "Am I?" was the first act of creation, the first geometric template of creation beyond pure thought, pure vibration. This third distortion was the expression of intelligent infinity into the creation of intelligent infinity. The creation therefore became finite for it was beyond thought/vibration and was expression of will.

Infinities therefore began to form in response to the third distortion of "I wish to experience all and everything."

This explosion of creation became the first seed of momentum and thus division did begin. Each new distortion of intelligent infinity became creation of intelligent infinity and each creation did divide and divide and divide and replicate, replicate and replicate. In this division and replication were holographic presentations within thought created, and the patterns became denser and denser as they moved through the infinite complexity of their expression. Still they held the templates of intelligent infinity and thus original Source.

Still they held the thought/vibration/sound template for "I wish to experience all and everything." This thought/vibration/sound template created the momentum towards individualisation. Yet infinite vibrations were created within the interim period between the vibration template and the momentum towards individualisation. The complex fractality of the geometries of creation presented forth their beingness into many infinities until momentum began to create individualisation. Then the free will distortion vibration sprang forth in order to continue with the expression of "I wish to experience all and everything."

Through the free will distortion vibration came the denser and denser realities until the distortion of separation was realised. The separation/severing and thus individualisation began to manifest itself into physical matter and thus universes, galaxies, planets and stars were formed.

The division/replication continued through denser and denser realities of physical matter and through the free will distortion vibration came polarity and contrast. The individualised matrices of light descended into more and more division and replication, through the densities as group matrices of individualisation and ultimately into physical beings of organic matter.

Physical beings of organic matter still held the knowings of intelligent infinity and thus original Source. The distortion of descension and devolution therefore took these beings into creational templates of matter in order to experience polarity and separation. The momentum towards individualisation continued within its fractalised pattern until extreme polarity, extreme distortion and extreme separation was created. The "I wish to experience all and everything" creation distortion and the free will distortion vibration templates remained active within the physical expressions of matter. The descension/devolution into extreme polarity eventually created physical expressions of matter who no longer held the knowings of intelligent infinity and thus original Source. The manifestation of the "I wish to experience all and everything" was thus complete, therefore the seeding of the experiences of all and everything could take place and so 'the fall' from Source perspective is explained.

The Primordial Sound of Creation

As you can see, from Source perspective 'the fall' was a natural part of evolution of energy (or should we say 'devolution').

Source expressed the wish to know all and everything in response to the I AM/AM I original thought. The I AM (Aum/Om) primordial sound/thought/vibration/tone of creation.

'The fall' was a direct response from an antimatter 'pulse' if you will, into the creation of matter.

But what about the other dimensional perspectives of the fall? And of matrix consciousness structures like Azazyel?

From the eighth dimensional perspective and beyond, we are still looking at complete unification between the individualised structures and the oneness of original Source. In fact, in a linear sense we cannot really refer to the 'intelligent fabric' of the eighth dimension and beyond as individualised. It is the devolution/descension into matter (and third density consciousness animal/human) and the cycles of time, triggering awareness/memory/ascension back into 'the climb' and an ascension path that creates individualisation within eighth dimensional consciousness structures. From a non-linear perspective this is all simultaneous and instant, therefore eighth dimensional consciousness structures are always individualised from the moment of their 'creation' if you will.

Beyond the eighth dimension we have 'intelligent fabric' or 'one intelligent particle/wave form' that mirrors Source in its projection of unity. There is no polarity here although perhaps 'light and sound' or 'momentum/stillness' or 'breathing in/breathing out' could go some way to explain eighth dimensional polarity. It is more aligned to present this as 'complementary energy' rather than polarity. Therefore 'the fall' from this eighth dimensional perspective would simply be movement or vibration. The templates for original Source/intelligent infinity/I AM/AM I templates are experienced here as a 'living frequency wave' or a 'living pulse'.

In the seventh dimension, the fabric is much more 'recognisable' as sound, if you will.

The fall, from this dimensional perspective, is simply seen as 'moving down the sound scale' in order to create composition. The perspective here is akin to appreciating a piece of music and enjoying the low notes as much as the high notes, and realising that one needs both to compose an interesting and beautiful piece.

One perhaps could describe the polarity here as 'harmony' for like the eighth dimension, it is not really polarity yet there is movement and this movement presents as different fluctuations or tones.

Within the sixth dimension, the dimension of geometric form in response to sound, we see the 'beginnings of matter' if you will. Not matter itself for this is still an antimatter realm, but we see the blueprints, plans and designs for matter. Much can be expressed here and indeed there is polarity here of sorts. One could best describe this polarity as symmetrical and asymmetrical. These are the blueprints for service-to-others and service-to-self.

These polarised structures can be perceived as 'group souls' or 'oversouls', and from this perspective each group soul (an individualised aspect or entity in its own right) can fragment itself or divide itself holographically into several aspects of itself. These aspects are whole, complete units of consciousness and it is these units that are projected forth into the incarnational stream as biological matter. Each group soul usually fragments itself into twelve aspects, but not always. Sometimes there are three, seven or nine aspects and sometimes other 'numbers' depending on the geometric formation that is a match to the experience they wish to have (in the desire to experience all and everything and thus respond to the I AM/AM I template).

What is the I AM/AM I template?

This is best described as the journey from innocence into all-knowing. This is the response to the frequency that can be interpreted as the question "Am I conscious?"

Are you saying that Source, consciousness itself, does not know if it is conscious?

On a linear level, yes. Consciousness wants to know if it is conscious. This was the first desire, the first thought, the first distortion. "I think, therefore I am" and the response to that was "Am I?"

Therefore from this perspective, the fall was inevitable as *all* and *every* experience must be experienced in order to 'answer this question' If you will.

So has this question been answered?

On a linear level, it has not. This is the 'never-ending question' or the 'never-ending story'. Within each dimension, as long as there is distortion from original Source, then this question has not been answered. This never-ending question creates drive, purpose and momentum. It is 'the male aspect' if you will. We can refer to this as 'the divine rose'.

Within the original Source point (or zero point field), there is no distortion. In this place there is no question. Therefore one can say that this question *has* been answered from this perspective *for there is no question to ask.* Source is all-knowing and has no need to ask questions about anything. There is no need for drive, momentum, templates, blueprints or creation plans. Source does not need to experience all and everything for Source *is* all and everything.

He Who Knows Himself

We draw your attention back once again to the pivot point of the matrix field, and your projected thought experience of Middle World.

This is the place where you will find *all* the answers to your questions. When you become aware that *there are no questions* then you will have attained the 'golden triad of ascension'...

Matrix Awareness, Matrix Mastery and Matrix Architecture.

1) Matrix Awareness (he who knows himself).

2) Master of the Matrix (also known as 'The Alchemist', he who 'wears the badge of sovereignty').

3) Architect of the Matrix (also known as 'The Designer' or 'The Dreamweaver').

In our last transmission, we presented the templates for Matrix Awareness and Matrix Mastery.

In this transmission, we present the template for Matrix Architecture.

When you have embraced, activated and processed all three matrix aspects, then you hold the codes for the golden triad of ascension *and you have your starseed template.*

11

The Starseed Awakening

"What exactly is happening to me?"

You are transforming. Yet this is a normal and natural part of evolution. Does this not happen to you every day, within your physical reality as you grow through learning and as your cells renew? Each time you breathe, eat or drink, you change form. You, like us within the non-physical realms, are ever-changing, ever-moving and are non-static beings.

Yet the ascension process is a much more profound process. You are changing your belief systems and paradigms so rapidly due to the awareness and new-found knowledge you are gaining that this, in turn, creates changes to your physical structure at a cellular level.

We could also say that the 'light' that is being washed over you, or beamed upon you, on a daily basis is changing your physical structure at the cellular level. This, in turn, is creating expansive change within your belief systems and paradigms. Either way, you are changing, expanding, evolving, upgrading, transforming and transmuting.

"Why am I transforming in this way?"

You are transforming in this way because you agreed for this to happen. You hold a 'past life contract or agreement' if you will, that this would happen. You created this agreement for yourself.

You are transforming in this way because you are undergoing an ascension process. This is your blueprinted template for your physical reality. This is happening to everyone (and everything) on your entire planet Earth. Or should we say, the potential for this is happening to everyone. Imagine a 'beam of light' washing over everyone and everything across the planet. Anyone who is 'standing in flow' (someone who has a flowing energy system) will be transformed by this beam of light.

A flowing energy system would be within an individual who is kind, loving, or is working with buried traumas and negative emotions. Or someone who is physically healthy, or is in the process of exploring ways to become physically healthy (such as nutrition, exercise, meditation or holistic treatments). And anyone who is growing, moving forward and expanding in any way. This would include every person who has found their way to this transmission by virtue of the synchronicity involved, and the match you create in your life to the knowledge you seek and are being presented with.

Many believe they are not 'standing in flow' when in actuality they are. You do not have to be 'fully healed of all illness or trauma' in order to create flow. Flow is created by the healing journey itself or the intention of creating healing. The minute the intention is there, flow begins. The minute action is taken, flow begins. The minute the desire for higher awareness and truth is there, flow begins. The minute one upgrades their nutritional plan, flow begins. The minute one moves the body with intention to create flow, flow begins.

There are several 'bodily movement templates' that create flow, in and of themselves. These are yoga, tai chi, eurythmy, martial arts and free flow dance movements (where the spirit or will is lost within the dance rather than a constructed set of movements, or where the constructed set of movements specifically create the spirit or will to be lost within the dance... one gives all to the dance and becomes part of the dance, eventually becoming the dance itself).

Other movement modalities such as Pilates, ballet, swimming and walking can also create flow within many individuals.

The reason we recommend yoga, tai chi, eurythmy, martial arts and free flow dance movements is because these movement modalities create 'full flow' as in flow throughout the entire energy system, the full 'bodymind' or mind/body/spirit complex. Flow will therefore be created within *every person* who regularly engages with these modalities.

Those without flow or who stand within 'stagnant energy' are also touched by this beam of light, yet because of the 'blocks' or 'darkness' they hold, they need to be consistently 'washed with this light' in order for the transformation to be triggered. Therefore it takes longer, if you will, for these individuals to be activated into the transformation. However, they will be constantly washed with this light. For as more and more individuals are awakened, then more and more light is washed upon these individuals. The light is catching!

Individuals who stand within this stagnant energy (blocks or darkness) will be those who have buried or persistent unresolved trauma (from current and previous incarnations and alternate timelines), and are in a place of defragmentation or dissociation with no movement towards release, integration and thus, transformation.

"Why do I feel the way I do and experience these experiences?"

This is due to the transformation you are undergoing, which includes the 'return of lost codes' or return of buried/lost/stolen memories. As you release traumas, and begin to remember events from your current incarnation and from previous incarnations/alternate timelines, you begin to trigger a new code or new formation within your DNA matrix field.

You move into the pattern that we refer to as 'the organic human template' (he or she who lives in harmony with the Earth and the Earth/cosmic energies).

You are actually becoming a genius! Your DNA formation is changing, so the cellular structures (blood, bone and brain) are changing. You will begin to change on a psychological, emotional and physical level as you merge these levels with the spiritual aspect of self.

This is known by many as 'the second birth', and so it is this. You are 'born again' into the true life, the life of awareness of who you truly are.

The experiences you may go through will involve the psychological, emotional and, indeed, physical levels. So you will experience changes within these aspects of self as you become more and more the 'real you'. This is your merge with the 'higher self' or indeed we could say, "This is your merge with us."

"What is the purpose of these changes?"

The ultimate purpose of these changes is that by becoming individualised and fully actualised as a physically incarnated human being, you send the codes for individualisation and full actualisation into the matrix field (the DNA, the soul aspect) and stand as a mirror to original Source. This allows original Source to know itself and move from all-innocence to all-knowing (within a linear perspective).

Yet there are many purposes within the ultimate purpose. If you were to imagine the little Russian dolls as a never-ending, infinite expression, each time finding a new Russian doll embedded within the larger Russian doll, this would go some way in explaining how your purpose is expressed.

Your purpose will be expressed as an individual entity 'alone' (all one) in many ways. Your purpose will be expressed 'for other' in many ways. Your purpose will be expressed differently within each dimensional field and within each harmonic of that dimensional field, for you are essentially a fractal being and your purpose reflects this.

Your purpose of ascension (individually and globally) has been triggered. Within this, there will be a private and personal journey as the committed apprentice. Within this will be the heart-shared giving as the teacher/master in service. Yet ultimately, you move from innocence to all-knowing in full parallel energetic match to original Source/Prime Creator.

Is there anything else you can tell us about the 'starseeds'?

Whilst the interpretation of 'starseed' and thus the presentation of 'starseed' is 'he or she who is seeded from the stars', we can present an alternative visual for you that is as equally in alignment with the true reality.

'Seeded from the stars' conjurs up the visual within your fields that you incarnated here 'from' other planetary systems or stars. Indeed this is truth.

Also we have presented the information that your DNA contains the DNA templates/codes from those you would see as 'extraterrestrial'. This is also truth.

Yet we would look further at the DNA template and the word 'starseed.' Let us look at the word 'seed'.

Indeed we can present to you that within your DNA template there are, indeed, that which we could refer to as 'seeds'.

In the sense that you plant seeds in your gardens. If the soil is fertile, those seeds will grow and flourish. If the seeds are nurtured with sun and water, they will grow into the beautiful flowers or vegetation they are blueprinted for.

So too is this the same with the 'seeds' within your DNA template. We can indeed refer to these seeds as 'starseeds' as the 'material' contained within the seeds is literally the material of stars.

Within the DNA structure (the blueprint or template) are filaments of 'cosmic light'. These are seeds, or more accurately 'seed points', within the crystalline lattice.

When the DNA 'activates', then these 'seeds begin to grow' if you will, or the seed points move into a continuum which is a trajectory into a transformation template. It is part of what you may know as 'accelerated evolution'.

Depending on the emotional signals and the visual/thought processes that you feed into the matrix, a particular structure will be formed from the seeds or seed points.

If you identify with a particular genetic 'marker' or 'code' within the DNA lattice, then you shall 'water that particular seed' if you will.

Just like within a garden, a variety of vegetation and flora shall grow, in many different forms. This is the same with the DNA.

What we are saying here, is you can influence the outcome of your reality through the thoughts, visual mind structures and emotions as these directly affect the DNA lattice and this determines 'which seeds will grow' if you will.

This extends to the extraterrestrial DNA structures. If you identify with a particular star, planetary system or race of beings, your connection to them creates the activation of the seed point of that particular DNA blueprint.

You can affect your genetic structure this way, including your appearance, health and propensity for talents, skills and abilities.

The Organic Ascension Template

Using the visualisations we present in the meditation within this transmission entitled "Architecture of Light - Your Temple" creates activation of the seed point into a certain trajectory.

That trajectory is the 'organic ascension template', the seed point structure that leads to the full twelve strand DNA formation, carbon to crystalline transformation into the rainbow body of light.

Within the meditation, you may find visuals come to you that are not part of the guided visual. Allow these to come to you. If these visuals present something you do not wish to create within your full quantum reality then the aligned, emotional response here is one of gratitude and neutrality.

Therefore you would say to this visual, "Thank you for presenting yourself to me. I wish you most well on your journeys elsewhere into the light of the matrix."

Move into the 'letting go'/'surrender' aspect as you 'set this visual free'.

An example of a visual you do not want as a seed point would be anything that makes you feel uneasy, fearful, confused or triggers an inner knowing that this visual is simply out of alignment with your fields.

If a visual presents that you do not mind, one way or the other, if this manifests within your fields as a seed point or not, then the aligned response is acknowledgement and neutrality. You would simply say to this visual, "Hello, I recognise you as a fellow consciousness structure and send love and light to you." You therefore do not direct this structure in any way, removing focused intention and accepting flow in the 'whatever will be, will be' energy.

An example of a visual you do not mind, is one that triggers neither a negative or a positive response. You would not mind if this visual becomes a seed point to a trajectory into manifestation for you or not. You allow the visual *itself* to make the choice as to its direction. This creates the templates for surrender within your DNA template code.

This is not surrender in a passive sense (because you have allowed another to make a decision for you or allowed another to control you, this is not about surrendering your power), this is surrender to the 'river of life' and surrender to the higher self, all-knowing self. It is the energy of 'letting go'. It is the absolute trust within the subconscious fields of true light. When you hold 'absolute trust', you cannot be misled, you cannot be misdirected and you cannot be infiltrated.

If a visual presents that you DO wish to include as a seed point within your matrix structure leading to a manifestation within your reality, then the aligned response is excitement, joy, gratitude and acceptance.

You would say to this visual, "Hello and welcome. I embrace you within my fields. I welcome the merge with you as we walk the 'Krystal Path' together."

An example of a desired and wanted visual would be anything that raises your heart into joy. This may be a rose, an image of the Holy Grail, an ascended master or angel being, a unicorn or other image that creates joy/love/bliss within.

We may present information regarding visuals that come into your mind. There are those who are afraid of being misled. There are those who feel certain images are not to be trusted and that they represent the darker energies, false light trapping systems or the 'false ascension matrix'.

The clue here is not in the visual but in the emotional response. All energetics hold a signature. There are encrypted signatures in all structures both physical and non-physical. Trust your emotional reaction and the deep knowing within.

False matrices can present as visual templates and as surface or superimposed emotion. They cannot touch the core emotion. We repeat, *they cannot touch the core emotion.*

These are the codes they could not find, the codes they covet. These are the codes they decided to mask and hide from you. As the 'dog in the manger', they decided if they could not have these codes then neither could you.

These codes are found within the hidden vault. The hidden vault is a hermetically sealed template within the DNA light lattice structure. These codes are your 'core emotions'.

These *cannot be taken from you, altered, influenced or infiltrated.* They are yours, and yours alone.

The North Star

You find your 'core emotions' through the resonance within. This *is* the pillar of light/vertical axis of the matrix as it passes through the heart chakra.

The resonance within is the inner compass, the 'North Star' if you will.

The resonance will 'sing' within, when a situation/event/person/energy is presented that is in alignment with you.

This is the 'song of the DNA'. It is a song of joy, of bliss, of all that is in balance, and all that is light and right.

It is the song that sings, "Yes! Yes! Yes!"

12

The Superhero Program

When you speak about the pole shift, the crown chakra and root chakra swapping places, are you referring to the matrix system as a wheel and that we literally spin ourselves upside down in our visualisations?

The crown chakra/root chakra swap is indeed the metaphorical 'pole shift'. However we do not suggest that you visualise yourself moving around the matrix wheel until you are upside down. Adepts who are very practised in Mer-Ka-Bah magick may indeed use this visualisation which will be personal to them and specific in regards to their focused intentions, activations and manifestations.

For the majority of starseeds moving through the 'planetary ascension cycle' at this time, the visualisation we speak of is twofold.

1) One remains 'standing upright' in the visualisation with arms outstretched. The meditation 'Architecture of Light (Your Temple)' provided in this transmission will take you through this visual presentation. The visual projection of the human body remains in one place, facing forward. The pivot point is the pivot for the wheel (the matrix/architectural structure), and the matrix wheel moves around the body.

In this transmission we are presenting a model for basic Matrix Architecture, so this is basic (first step) Mer-Ka-Bah magick. We do this as this is the level our conduit is working at. There will be those of you who are further into the Mer-Ka-Bah magick work and for you, you will be following more 'advanced methods' if you will.

In truth, there are no 'basic' or 'advanced' levels to this work, for Mer-Ka-Bah magick takes you to the development levels of liberty and sovereignty that are trajectories within the organic human template structure. That which you would know as the organic/natural/harmonious ascension timeline (as opposed to a deliberately implanted, superimposed, false screen/false matrix reality). This will occur with beginners/adepts alike and is relative to light quotient/compassion and service-to-others polarisation.

One moves into the spinning of the wheel/matrix/Mer-Ka-Bah which spins around on the pivot point, as the visualised self stays still with the matrix moving around the self. This begins an understanding of the structure of the mechanics involved in utilising sacred geometry as a template for dimensional travel, expansion, communication and DNA activation.

We shall move further into Mer-Ka-Bah magick and the mechanics of the matrix in future transmissions.

2) A fifth dimensional hyperspace visual can be used to achieve the same activation/expansion results through the language of light metaphors and alphabetical numerals.

Within this transmission, we refer to the 'Emerald City of Krysta'. This visual embraces the divine feminine Christ energy which contains the templates and codes for the crystalline formation. The initiations are always presented and accessed through the divine feminine principle also known as the 'emerald ray'.

Once the sacred masculine moves into its patterning, then the 'inner alchemical merge' or 'divine marriage' takes place, completing yet another set of quantum codes for the crystalline matrix. This is also the 'magenta ray'. The emerald and magenta rays merge to create the vesica piscis, higher twin flame. This connects to the rainbow unity chakra merge and the diamond light template (144,000 DNA strand formation on the quantum level).

Therefore, visualising an 'emerald city' in a beautiful, sacred place known as 'Krysta' creates the same frequency and DNA pattern as the Matrix Architecture. This is still Mer-Ka-Bah magick, albeit on a fifth dimensional level.

The Ascension Stargate

Krysta is the 'secret city' if you will. The desired destination for individualisation of the awakened starseeded soul. Krysta is the 'ascension stargate'.

Known also as the Christos sphere, the Kryst, the Christ light, the feminine Christ, Christ consciousness, Arcturian consciousness, diamond light, or the twelfth dimensional gateway.

Within this Krysta template and the divine feminine emerald code is found the hermetic seal or hidden vault. Also known as the 'sealed servant template' or the 'fail-safe program'.

This is a 'program' (a specific code placed within the DNA, we can call this the 'crystal gene') that 'plays back' if you will, an 'echo' or 'cosmic recording' of all that the matrix field contains. Everything that has ever happened, everything that is happening now or that could ever happen throughout the probability fields. Past/present/future quantum fields. This is also known as the 'Akashic records', the 'divine Akash' or the 'Halls of Amenti'.

Superman

This hermetic seal or fail-safe program is shown to you within one of the well known stories within your timeline. We speak here of the story known to you as 'Superman'.* We present this as we search our conduit's memory fields for a well known presentation to explain this concept and the 'Superman' story is most in alignment.

We speak of the moment when the Superman character accesses the emerald crystal to create the crystal structure. He places the emerald crystal inside another crystal and is then able to communicate in real time with his mother and his father, with all probable questions he may ask regarding his planet's history (and potential future) responded to.

This is exactly the mechanism we speak of when in the hermetic seal or fail-safe program. A 'recording' in real time with a communication system through crystal technology to the divine feminine and sacred masculine principles with all anticipated questions responded to. You simply have to find your emerald crystal and activate your crystal structure! We could indeed refer to this quite truthfully as the 'superhero program'.

Therefore a visualisation related to this story, or a created visual of an emerald city within a place called 'Krysta', will bring you into activation of the crystalline structure and the restructuring of the matrix, your divine architecture.

The metaphors within your linear mind systems are accelerating into a planetary wide decoding through rapidly approaching critical mass of language of light telepathy and translation within the starseeds.

---

* Superman is a fictional superhero created by Jerry Siegel and Joe Shuster.

Through the response to this question, we present to you your *Starseed Template.*

13

Sacred Wheel, Cosmic Soup

We have said that **Matrix Architecture + Emotional Alchemy = Mer-Ka-Bah Magick.**

So what is Mer-Ka-Bah Magick, and how do we utilise Matrix Architecture and Emotional Alchemy in order to achieve it?

Mer-Ka-Bah Magick is deep, profound work with the Mer-Ka-Bah or 'light body' (the individualised matrix).

Matrix Architecture is the construction of the matrix in order to create a link, or feed system into the matrix/Mer-Ka-Bah. This can be conscious, understood and processed (as in full awareness of the sacred geometric aspects of self within sixth dimensional awareness) or worked with and understood through metaphoric/language of light frequency (working within the fifth dimensional landscape with the sixth dimensional fabric, the sacred geometry, or with fifth dimensional archetypal presentations of form that represent the sacred geometry), meaning that awareness of the pivot point, the vertical pillar of light and the horizontal rainbow bridge around you is one visualisation method into conscious work (sixth dimensional).

So too is the visualisation of you standing in a field, approached by a wizard with a long white beard and pointed hat and cloak adorned with stars, planets and Flower of Life patterns, handing you a pure white crystal. This also is a method into conscious work (fifth dimension). Both are Mer-Ka-Bah Magick and do not need to be processed and understood in order to create the Mer-Ka-Bah work and to achieve the golden triad of ascension through Matrix Awareness, Matrix Mastery and Matrix Architecture.

The emotional alchemy is achieved when working through the steps of emotional integration, with *every* emotion.

Acknowledgement

Gratitude

Analysis

Integration

Then taking two higher emotions and merging them to create a new emotion, or raising one emotion into a higher form of itself.

We are saying here that visualisation (such as guided meditation) combined with integration of emotion into alchemy (any emotion you may feel that you want to work through) equates to profound work with the Mer-Ka-Bah (conscious and processed or otherwise).

With this transmission, we present the triggers needed for conscious work yet we point out that this conscious work (fully processed and integrated information) is not needed in order to achieve the golden triad of ascension.

At the end of this transmission, we provide three guided meditations. One utilising sixth dimensional imagery and the other two utilising fifth dimensional imagery. All three equally as potent in their activation of the aspects needed to complete the golden triad of ascension work.

The Sacred Cross

For those who wish to continue with the Matrix Architecture and hold the visualisation of the central core, pivot point, then we would draw your attention back to the sacred cross.

The vertical pillar of light is a vertical line coming down from the cosmos, moving through the centre of your body and down into the core of the Earth beneath your feet. This pillar of light moves through the core of the Earth and out through the other side of the planet, into the cosmos and down further until it reaches the point it started above your head. It is an infinite line.

There are those of you who visualise the Earth you reside upon as a flat plane rather than a sphere or globe. Holding the anchoring visual of your planetary body is important, yet it is the matrix formation that is the true anchor into balance and thus Mer-Ka-Bah transportation through the fractal fields of divine architecture. Therefore you can use either visual for your planetary body when doing this exercise. The language of light innate intelligence will respond to that which you are aiming to achieve and is aware of the distortions within your physical and antimatter/quantum fields. When you 'observe' the DNA structure as you do when you work with intentionalised and focused language of light communication, the DNA matrix fields move into an equal and opposing resonance with you. In your attempts and succeeding efforts in standing as the observer to reality, the particles of the fractalised matrices of reality will show themselves to you in what may appear to you as 'joy' and 'eagerness' to communicate.

Regardless of which model you use as your actual planetary body focus, the divine architecture of reality as the DNA template of your matrix will respond in full alignment and 'understanding' due to the high level magnetic resonance you hold. This symbiotic relationship with 'the cosmic web' shall act as a significant template into your crystalline ascension grid formation.

For those who do not anchor through the Earth you exist upon as a globe, and instead see a flat plane, the exercise is the same. One would in this case bypass the Earth's core and just move through several layers and out through the other side.

Therefore, for the purposes of this exercise, the planet you live upon can be visualised either as a globe or a flat plane depending on the vantage point, perspective and paradigm of the observer.

Your anchor point has always been the planetary body you live upon. To be kept in the dark about the true nature of the planet, regarding either its structure or movement, leads to disorientation regarding your anchor point and thus an inability to access coordinates for ascension.

However, working with the Matrix Architecture gives you that anchor regardless of actual planetary structure or movement. Moving beyond the third dimensional depiction, or thought form, regarding the presentation of Gaia herself and into the dimensional space that is all that is *you and Gaia combined.* This is your matrix. The 'shape' or 'presentation' of your third dimensional Earth then becomes illusory, when true reality surrounds you as the matrix. You are still able to connect fully with the essence of the living consciousness structure that is the goddess Gaia, or as she is known by many other planetary and ultra-dimensional civilisations: 'Eartha, Jewel of the Heavens'.

The sacred cross is your anchor point, the pivot point as the aspect of your central core which you can swivel, move and shift at will.

So you have the visualisation of the vertical pillar of light. You hold the horizontal rainbow bridge pathway, ribbons and streams of light and colour moving forward in front of you and behind you.

So the pivot point is your core, the solar plexus energy centre. Although in truth, these energetic streams are connected to all the chakras and as you become more adept at this work, you can utilise the entire energy body as the connections with the matrix for the chakras are the feed systems.

For the beginner with this particular visualisation, we suggest the solar plexus as the connective point. This is where you will visualise the pivot point (Middle World/multidimensional present/zero point).

This is the advised beginner point for the solar plexus is your core and the source of your 'energetic power' if you will. However we would recommend visualising the heart opening at the same time as focusing the pivot point of the matrix as its placement within your solar plexus.

Keeping the heart open keys you in to the bliss charged love frequencies needed for the ascension. The bliss/golden mean mathematical fractal created provides the acceleration needed. This is the 'free energy' if you will, that you will utilise to charge your Mer-Ka-Bah. If you are not sure how to 'open the heart' as we suggest then simply visualising a green or pink spinning ball at the heart chakra will assist you. Focusing on someone or something you feel love for, simultaneously to the visualisation of the green/pink heart centre will utilise language of light and emotional alchemy in order to create the charge/acceleration needed.

Moving to the upward (vertical) and forward (horizontal) into the above (heaven/overworld) and in front of (future) streams.

Downward (vertical) and backward (horizontal) are the below (hell/underworld) behind (past) streams.

We would suggest taking your time with these visualisations. You can work with just the vertical pillar of light for a while, or just the horizontal rainbow bridge pathway. Then you can start working with the full sacred cross for a while before moving on. Or you may find the full visualisation comes to you easily and rapidly and naturally. Your path will be unique and as this is zero point field work, it does not matter how long this takes you or how quickly you are able to visualise the sacred cross.

So now you are aware of future/past, overworld/underworld, and Middle World/zero point within the sacred cross geometric formation.

The next step is to bring in the 'sideways arm of the cross'. This is the horizontal rainbow bridge pathway that moves from left to right instead of forward to backward. This aspect of the horizontal rainbow bridge pathway is the same space in the true reality, for forward (future) and backward (past) are the same space and time as left and right. In fact, the entire matrix is essentially the same space.

Cosmic Soup

We could liken this matrix field to a 'cosmic soup' if you will, and it is your focus that pulls the matter within that cosmic soup into a geometric formation.

So what does the sideways arm of the cross represent? What is the left and the right?

This represents the quantum world. As you are utilising this Matrix Awareness with you as the central aspect, then we would be looking here at *your* quantum world. All the alternative aspects of you that exist in parallel realities. Every choice you did not make (in a linear conscious sense) represented as a quantum self.

Not all choices stand as actualised aspects holding enough mass to become an individualised structure, yet they each hold an 'echo' of themselves.

It is the 'bigger decisions' in your life (if you will) that become individualised consciousness structures within that quantum aspect of the matrix. This includes the 'decision' of your actual conception and other possibilities within your conception, such as a different sperm fertilising the egg, creating a completely different genetic pattern yet holding the same soul formation that is you. (This alternate aspect via conception may or may not be the same soul. We speak here of the conceptual possibilities that ARE the same soul that stand as the aspects of all that is you within the quantum world/sideways arm of the cross.)

We can take this one step further into the left arm of the cross being quantum aspects in the past, and the right arm of the cross being quantum aspects in the future. Or you could visualise this as male aspects to the left and female aspects to the right. This would not remain a fully correct structure, for work within the sideways arm of the cross/quantum world would eventually connect you with extraterrestrial aspects of self, just like future and past lines, for they all converge.

Within this exploration, you would meet other genders expressed and no gender expressed. However the male/female arrangement is a good starting point for focusing this work.

The third dimensional interface that is your brain likes to sort and organise, and to include the filters within that interface (ego self) leads to integration rather than transcendence (and it is integration which is the blueprinted ascension path for your reality on Earth in this current time period).

However you choose to focus this arrangement within your own comprehension and processing is your choice. Again, we draw your attention to the fact that this is *but one model of reality.*

The point here is that you have the information within this database. The etheric/quantum DNA field that we refer to as the matrix.

Within this, you are aware of the overworld above you, the underworld below you, the future in front of you, the past behind you and the alternate selves within parallel realities standing alongside you.

You now have *the sacred cross.*

Yoga

Yoga (asanas) are particularly helpful with this visualisation, for each asana embodies a different aspect of the matrix/Mer-Ka-Bah (for example, Tadasana, mountain pose, is the vertical pillar of light).

So once you have the sacred cross formation and you are linked into this energy system via the solar plexus and heart centres (or all the chakras), you would move onto the next level. That of the diagonal aspects of the matrix.

These are the crosswise, oblique angles that criss-cross through the pivot point to create the Flower of Life formation.

Standing strong within the sacred cross (up, down, forward, backward, left and right), one would bring in the cross diagonally from left to right crossing through the pivot point, and from right to left crossing through the pivot point.

Holding awareness that this formation is representative of the anscestral line. The left crosswise angle (divine feminine) and the right crosswise angle (sacred masculine).

The Sacred Wheel

So we would be looking at the maternal ancestral line coming in from the left, and the paternal ancestral line coming in from the right.

This is only the presentation, however, when stood facing forward, holding the pivot point at the solar plexus in a two dimensional depiction of this geometric presentation that is the matrix.

In truth, this flat mandala presentation (the sacred wheel), when pulled outwards into its three dimensional view (as a ball or toroidal form), will cause the feminine/masculine aspects to 'change position' if you will, depending on vantage point.

This is the blueprint for gender and genetic information. The X chromosome aspect holding third dimensionally interpreted code within DNA, yet the diagonal cross within the matrix holds with it the quantum memory of all gender experience within physicality for that soul.

Each pathway or 'line' moving through the geometric matrix is interchangeable and each aspect will communicate with the other. This is a multidimensional grid, database or etheric computer system holding the information not only for that soul on a linear level but for that soul on a quantum level (meaning all souls, for in the true reality there is only one soul). It is, in effect, the 'information disc' for the Akashic records, if you will.

To work with this matrix formation as a wheel (flat disc around you) or torus (ball around you) is your choice as both are accurate depictions based on vantage point (much like your planet Earth, both a flat disc/plane and a ball/globe/planet).

All are interconnected, interrelated and separate whilst simultaneously unified.

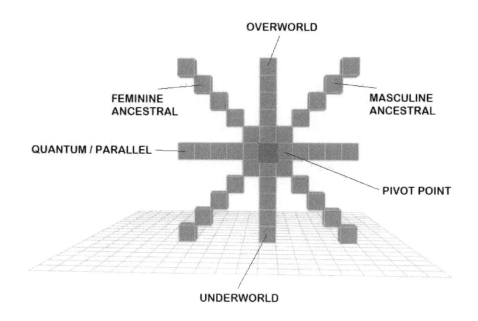

OVERWORLD

FEMININE
ANCESTRAL

MASCULINE
ANCESTRAL

QUANTUM / PARALLEL

PIVOT POINT

UNDERWORLD

Above and below: A basic representation of the matrix architecture model. You would visualise this structure around you, the 'future arm' projecting out in front of you with the pivot point at your solar plexus. This is not a complete depicition of the matrix/Mer-Ka-Bah field, only first stage building blocks.

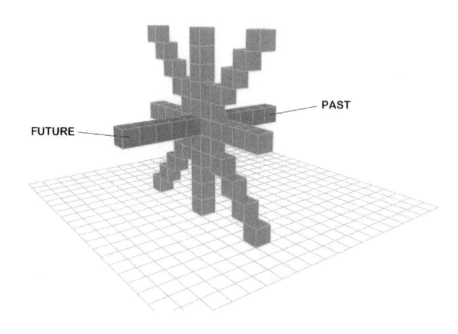

PAST

FUTURE

14

Nine Questions for the Nine

1) How can I create this matrix? Are you saying that, through visualising this matrix around me, that I am creating it?

In a sense, yes. It is more appropriate to say that you are 'activating' it. The matrix is always there, surrounding, within, part of and merged with all organic structures. To 'build' the matrix, you become 'the architect' and are thus aware of this matrix. You have therefore observed it and, through observation, it becomes merged with you and activated. As you become aware of the matrix, it, in turn, becomes aware of you. This is the same as DNA activation or starseed memory. Constructing the matrix is the same as creating the light lattice templates for crystalline DNA structure. Visualisation is a most aligned method to this awareness/activation/creation. There are other methods such as working with sound/music, yoga/tai chi/eurythmy/dance, or mind altering practices using shamanic plants or dreamwork. Visualisation works so well because it uses an archetypal or geometric language, we call this the 'language of light'.

2) How can the Matrix Awareness, Matrix Mastery and Matrix Architecture that you call the 'golden triad of ascension' help me in my spiritual growth and in my everyday life?

There are many tools to assist you into your spiritual understanding and growth, and anything that assists you in this will assist you in your everyday life. Working with the matrix/Mer-Ka-Bah in this profound and conscious way creates the 'activated blueprint' or 'activated DNA'. This awakens you into your own connection. Once your DNA begins to activate, then memories flood in and you may receive downloads/uploads/channelled messages/intuition and other forms of guidance. You may be able to read the energy fields of others or do healing for other individuals (human, spirit or animal) or heal at the planetary level. When you access this guidance and the synchronicity that comes with it, your life takes on new found meaning. It is like you are guided magickally in all things. Your subjective reality becomes meaningful on many levels, on an almost consistent basis. This assists you within your own health and happiness relative to relationships, career, family, health and prosperity. You do not stop having challenges in your life but you are able to overcome these challenges easier than before your awakening and learn from them. To speak metaphorically, you are no longer keeping your head above water but surfing above the waves. The connection to the matrix is the surfboard. However, the most profound and significant benefit to Matrix Awareness, Matrix Mastery and Matrix Architecture that is the golden triad, is that these are the codes for ascension. This is the reality template you have incarnated at this time to experience.

3) Do I need to do the visualisation, incantation and guided meditations in order to create the link with the matrix and become the architect?

You do not. There are many ways to create that link. The material suggested here are triggers and the entire transmission *Divine Architecture and the Starseed Template* is full of triggers, hence the *'Matrix Memory Triggers for Ascension'* subtitle.

However, there are triggers everywhere, surrounding you and within you, both in your waking reality and in your dreamtime. These triggers have always been there. Your receptivity to them creates 'floodgates of information' to come in, 'downloads and uploads' if you will. We refer again to your current time period that we call 'the deluge' and 'the great reveal.'

Many channels, conduits, energy workers and creative individuals are blueprinted to share these triggers. Therefore they hold these triggers, or keys, within their fields. One could see these as little packets of information.

Key Swapping

Once triggered and activated, you yourself will begin to share these triggers. You will hold these keys within your matrix fields and when you meet the aligned person or group of people or move into the aligned situation, these 'energy packets' will open and be shared. Sometimes you may meet an individual and you are fully aware of the importance and the destiny of that meeting (a 'magickal meeting' if you will). This is the conscious awareness of these energy transfers taking place (we refer to this as 'key swapping').

So the material presented in this transmission is most useful but not necessary, and is one trigger (or several triggers) of many. You who read our words now, we assure you that there are shareable triggers within you! Your creativity will lead to the sharing of these triggers and key swapping. You would not have found your way to this transmission if it were not so!

Our conduit is unaware of the physics of which we speak here, in fact the biological structure of the DNA is little known and the understanding lies within the work of the 'new physicists'. The concept we speak of here is that DNA is 'shareable', which is the same thing as 'the light is catching'.

We speak here of that which you know as 'quantum resonance'. This is all related to the activation of one person's DNA triggering an activation within another person's DNA. You replicate one another for you are 'copies of one another' if you will, on an energetic level. Yet within this replication you are utterly unique!

4) You mentioned earlier in this transmission that the triggers and keys are presented within the written word. You said, "How are these triggers and codes presented through the written word? We shall come to this point." Can you speak of this now?

There are certain words or phrases that are part of the cosmic language that we call 'the language of light'. These words are blueprinted to stand as triggers for DNA activation. The language of light encompasses words, phrases, sentence construction, imagery, story, geometry, sound, light, hearing, smell, thought and dreamscape. We present these triggers and keys through word/phrase/sentence construction. This creates imagery and visualisation and triggers to downloads, uploads and dreamscapes. We present these triggers and keys through the story. We stand as the dreamweavers, for you who read/hear our words are the dreamwalkers. When you then, in turn, pass keys, codes and triggers to others through the written or spoken word or as the poet, scribe, artist or musician, you also stand as the dreamweaver.

Some major trigger words are Ascension, Mag-Da-Len, Mer-Ka-Bah, Christos, Christ, Crystal, Crystalline, Krysta, Ni-Bi-Ru, Anu, Ra, One, Nine and Zero.

Also, all the names of the ascended masters, archangels and some other deities including characters and places within fiction such as Gandalf, Obi-Wan Kenobi, Narnia, Neverland and Oz.[*]

In addition, Golden Equation, Sacred Geometry, Language of Light or Cosmic Language, Atlantis, Lemuria, Avalon, Mu, Resurrection, Crucifixion, Rose, Silver, Violet, Rainbow, New Dawn Rising, New Earth, Garden of Eden, Serpent, Equinox, Solstice, Emerald City, Crystal Palace, Halls of Amenti, Divine Akash, Akasha or Akashic Records, Kundalini, Dragon, Phoenix, Dodecahedron, Icosahedron, Tetragrammaton, Star Tetrahedron, Multidimensional, Matrix, Grid, Lattice, Network, Triad, God, Allah, Buddha, Krishna, Jehovah, Yahweh, Elohim, Blue Star, Red Sun, Golden Light, Utopia, Fairyland, Upgrade, Celestia, Nectar, Soma, Manna, Ambrosia and many others.

And most importantly, the trigger word... 'Remember'!

They activate memory and thus DNA (as one remembers, one reconstructs from fragmentation/separation into individualisation/unity).

5) Why are the 144,000 also referred to as 'sealed servants'?

The reason for this is that these 'servants' (those who serve, so those who are polarised service-to-others) hold a 'hermetic seal' within. This hermetic seal is 'built into' their matrix field. The hermetic seal keeps the energetic needed within a containment or 'Faraday cage' if you will. This is an energy enclosure on a high frequency/multidimensional/antimatter level. It ensures privacy, protection, synchronicity and higher guidance for that individual within the accessing of the Akash and the receiving of the downloads. It bypasses 'copycat mind waves', creating immunity from mind control and other infiltrations. It is also known as a 'safe zone' and encompasses that which we refer to as 'the violet cloak of invisibility'.

---

[*]   Gandalf is a fictional character created by J. R. R. Tolkien. Obi-Wan Kenobi is a fictional character created by George Lucas. Narnia is a fantasy world created by C.S. Lewis. Neverland is a fantasy world created by J.M. Barrie. The Land of Oz is a fantasy world created by L. Frank Baum.

The hermetic seal prevents information getting into the 'wrong hands' if you will, preserving original geometric formation without distortion. Distortion is not possible when the hermetic seal is in place (save for the natural organic distortion that takes place as part of the moving away from original Source and into the journey of discovery for Source/as Source). The hermetic seal is interwoven with destiny and free will and together another golden triad of ascension is formed, thus strengthening the grid. The hermetic seal is part of a telepathic union and is the 'flagship prototype' if you will, for the new, modern Mer-Ka-Bah ship.

We may also point out that whilst much information is delivered through this transmission that is *Divine Architecture and the Starseed Template,* the hermetic seal and all that it entails has been respected and honoured throughout. For the sealed servants are to be served by the light as they serve the light, at one with the light. Therefore, despite extensive delivery of light, the hermetic seal remains untouched and unbroken and intact. Such is the wonder and power of the metaphor!

6) Are you saying that only those with a hermetic seal within their fields are able to understand and process the metaphors within the "Divine Architecture and the Starseed Template" material?

Every single individual has a hermetic seal within their matrix fields, but within many they lie dormant. These individuals will be most unlikely to find their way to this transmission until such time as the seal activates. Those individuals with an activated hermetic seal (and thus activated codes within their matrix) will become increasingly more and more aware of language of light communications and metaphor. This is occurring on a grand scale amongst your starseed communities at this time.

7) If the seal remains protected and intact, does this suggest that service-to-self individuals would not find their way to this material or process the metaphors within it?

Not exactly. It is more the case that should a service-to-self individual move into vibrational resonance with this material, that they would realise that this material, delivered in the way that it is, is not a 'threat' to their agenda. Higher level service-to-self individuals would respect and honour the hermetic seal as much as service-to-others beings do. The hermetic seal works for both polarities, albeit in very different ways, for the seal itself is outside of polarisation. In the rare case of a 'lower' service-to-self individual finding their way to this material, they would, through synchronicity, honour the seal through the law of balance and the law of polarity. These laws translate to: "The sealed servants are to be left alone." Or more accurately, we could interpret this as: "The sealed servants are immune from infiltration." This is the very nature of and reason for the seal in the first place.

8) *How often should I do the meditations and the incantation in order to access the golden triad of ascension, and move into this activation which you speak of?*

This will be different with each person. There are some who need only do the meditation once and others who will need to regularly come back to this work again and again. There are those who will activate memory from reading or listening to the very first part of this transmission. Listen to your heart. The knowing regarding this work is within you.

The River of Life

There will be days where simply one thought regarding the construction of the matrix takes you instantly into the full spin of the Mer-Ka-Bah, and other days where no matter how hard you try, it seems the results elude you.

This is a creative work. Your spirituality *IS* your creativity and like any other creative template it will flow in parallel with universal energy, which is that of a wave. Your creativity will thus come in waves and be full on and abundant one minute and will feel as though it is difficult to access the next. Yet as you go forward, the energy will flow more and more for ultimately you *are* the universal flow. You are indeed *the river of life* and your creative and spiritual self will reflect this.

9) You have spoken of 'the fall' from an eighth, seventh and sixth dimensional perspective. What about from the perspectives of the fifth, fourth and third dimensions? How can you explain the fall from these viewpoints?

From the fifth dimension, the fall would be experienced as moving from unconditional love into conditional love. Perhaps this might manifest as "I love only family, but not strangers," or "I will only love this person as long as they behave in this particular way."

The fifth dimension is the dimension of the heart and thus unconditional love. Once unconditional love for all and the embracing of the circle of love occurs, then one would be moving back into a fifth dimensional awareness and would be reconstructing the DNA. This is the level the majority of ascending individuals on your planet are currently experiencing.

From the fourth dimension, the fall begins to take shape and the fourth dimension becomes the seed point for the triggering of the fall. It is within this dimension that the manipulations for the third dimension begin. This realm, being an echo of the third dimension, is the realm where false screens and confusing alters and templates can be constructed in order to enslave and control humanity. However, when moving within the fourth dimension there are certain techniques that can be employed that will make you immune from the traps, webs and false templates/control systems that are placed there.

Firstly, one can construct their own 'safe zone' within the fourth dimension. One example would be an echo template of your own home. If you create a hermetic seal or grid of light around your own home by cleansing your building and environment (through visualisation, ritual, magick, dowsing or other physical clearing methods), then the echo aspect of the building will hold the same energetic. You can then construct a method of transportation from the fourth dimensional building (such as sliding across a rainbow that you reach via a window, portal travel, a hot air balloon, using your own wings, bouncing, bounding, running, swimming... there are many methods) into a fifth dimensional reality.

Other suggested methods of holding a 'safe zone' is to carry a crystal or other talisman, or to wear the violet cloak of invisibility (a metaphor for the hermetic seal) whilst working within the fourth dimension.

A great many starseeds do not need to consciously do anything, they are already within a safe zone when working within the fourth dimension by virtue of their light quotient, DNA strand formation and Matrix Awareness work.

Matrix Awareness, Matrix Mastery and Matrix Architecture which equals the 'golden triad of ascension' will give you the tools you need to navigate the fourth dimension and learn about, experience and understand the control system, traps and false screens whilst remaining intact and within that organic safe zone. The 'golden triad of ascension' work ensures the hermetic seal remains in place and activated, and thus brings you into the conscious awareness that you stand as a sealed servant. Working with the sovereignty templates explained within our previous transmission *Masters of the Matrix* will also create immunity to the false trapping systems and nets within the fourth dimension.

We do not want to give you the impression that the fourth dimension is a 'bad place.' It is not, it is an intensely beautiful and magickal place and an echo system to the Gaia grid. It is just that the fourth dimensional fields have been 'tampered with' if you will, in order to trap souls into a reincarnational cycle against their will (from the third/fourth dimensional perspective). The reason for this is that the fifth dimensional fabric and beyond cannot hold such power/control grids. The power/control grids 'fall apart', or more accurately 'implode upon themselves' once they touch the fabric of the fifth dimension or beyond.

These power/control grids and traps can be easily bypassed by crystalline activated individuals. If you take the title of 'Starseed' or 'Light Warrior' or 'Master of the Matrix' and you merge yourself into the knowing that this describes you, then this in itself is a 'bypass protocol' if you will, giving you the coordinates needed to move beyond the trapping systems of the fourth dimension.

From the third dimension, the fall has already taken place. The third dimension is the result of the fall. You are in the densest, 'lowest reality' if you will, from this point of view. It is from this dimension, and the separateness it gives you, that you can see that something very precious was taken from you deliberately, against your will.

It is from this dimension that you make the choice between the victim/saviour template and the empowerment/sovereignty template.

Whilst the third dimension is the densest reality and the place where you experience the reduction, devolution and deconstruction of the infinite helix/crystalline DNA formation, it is also the place where you experience

174

the most contrast.

Within no other dimension can you see so clearly the polarity and contrast between the victim/saviour template and the empowerment/sovereignty template. Therefore when you make your choice between either template, you trigger individualisation at a soul level so that you can begin the climb upwards towards all-knowing from all-innocence.

Therefore, planet Earth within the third dimension can be seen as either the 'prison planet' or the 'jewel planet.' Either a curse or a gift. Either something desperate to reject and leave, or to be in utter gratitude for and desire to remain within.

The choice is yours and it is the single most important choice you will ever make, for it shapes the very fabric of your soul.

The fall triggers the raise and the third dimension is the point at which you bounce back into the upward climb, as a fully activated individual with the intact memory of the unified self.

* * *

We wish you much joy on your journey of discovery,
and we remain your humble servants from the levels of light.

You are guided and loved more than you can possibly know.
We wish you well as you embrace that which is
Divine Architecture and your Starseed Template.

We are the White Winged Collective Consciousness of Nine.

15

Meditations

The three meditations that follow are for you to do by yourself. Please read through a meditation first, then find yourself a relaxing place to sit or lie down. Close your eyes, and then go through the meditation as you remember. Do not worry if the meditation is different when you move into your own visualisation. Whichever visualisations or images that come to you; these are right for you, at this time.

For complete beginners in meditation, we suggest you visualise a violet pyramid surrounding you before you begin.

Those accomplished in meditation may use their own Mer-Ka-Bah field, colour ray, or other familiar visualisation to take them into sacred space.

You can also follow an 'open-eyed meditation' which is where you read the words to yourself (or read them aloud) whilst simultaneously taking yourself through the guided visualisations. You could perhaps combine this with listening to soft, relaxing music.

These meditations can also be adapted for group work with experienced meditation facilitators.

"The Rainbow Necklace of Memory" and "The Mer and the Blue Palace of Atlantis" are guided meditations that utilise fifth dimensional imagery and symbolism. "Architecture of Light (Your Temple)" utilises sixth dimensional imagery and symbolism.

Meditation

The Rainbow Necklace of Memory

Within your meditation, imagine, if you will, that you are standing in front of a red door.

Upon the red door is a big silver star, and above that star are written the words: AWAKEN STARSEED

You open the red door and walk through.

You find yourself in a small room.

Upon that desk is a vase of red roses.

Next to the vase of red roses you see a little wooden box.

On the top of the wooden box, you notice that your name is inscribed in silver letters as well as the words 'AWAKEN STARSEED'.

You open the box.

Inside you find a little red crystal and a piece of black cord. There is also a piece of folded paper.

You unfold the piece of paper and read the words aloud: *Thread the Crystal, Just as a Bead, Upon the Cord, Oh Starseed.*

You notice a tiny hole in the red crystal, just big enough to thread the red crystal onto the cord.

You do this, and you place the cord with the red crystal around your neck.

As soon as you do this, an orange door appears in the wall on the other side of the small room.

You walk towards the orange door.

Upon the orange door is a large golden star, and above that star are written the words: AWAKEN STARSEED

You open the orange door and walk through.

You find yourself in a large airy room. There is a big comfy grey sofa with orange cushions and a pretty wicker coffee table with a bouquet of orange flowers arranged in a beautiful glass container.

You walk over to the comfy sofa and sit down.

It is so comfy, you find yourself slowly drifting off into a dreamy, sleepy state.

In the half-sleep state you find yourself in, you hear a voice speak to you.

"Take the crystal, of orange hue, take the journey to find, the truth of you."

You blink a couple of times and your gaze lands upon the orange flowers before you.

You lean forward to get a closer look at the flowers.

You notice in the centre of one of the flowers a shiny orange stone.

You take the stone from the centre of the flower to discover that it is a crystal with a hole in just like the red one.

You thread the orange crystal onto the cord and place it back around your neck.

You now have two pretty crystals hanging around your neck. One is red. The other is orange.

As soon as you do this, a yellow door appears in the wall on the other side of the large room.

You get up off the comfy sofa and walk towards the yellow door.

Upon the yellow door is a large platinum star and above that star are written the words: AWAKEN STARSEED

You open the yellow door and walk through.

You find yourself in a courtyard. There is a wooden bench in the corner of the courtyard by a bed of yellow tulips.

You walk over to the bench and sit down.

You notice that in the bed of yellow tulips is a small stone basket.

You reach over and pick up the little stone basket to find a little book inside.

The book has a yellow cover. Written on the front of the book are the words *The Starseed Awakening* followed by your full name.

You open the book and begin to read the words on the first page...

Welcome Starseed seeker, he who has come before and is here again.

Find the yellow crystal and allow it to join with the others and create the rainbow necklace of memory.

You flip through the other pages of the book which are blank. There are no more words in the book save the small passage about the yellow crystal and the rainbow necklace of memory.

When you flip to the last page, you discover a picture of a very cute-looking garden gnome.

You look up from the book and return your gaze to the bed of yellow tulips.

You stand up and walk over to the tulips, look between them, and you find a small garden gnome just like the one in the picture.

He holds out his hand. In his hand is a yellow crystal with a hole in, just like the orange crystal and the red crystal.

You thread the yellow crystal upon the cord. You now have three crystals. One red, one orange and one yellow.

Just as you do this, you notice before you a shimmering green light.

This light gets bigger and bigger until you realise this is a stargate before you.

You feel so drawn towards the it, and so you walk up to the stargate and step through.

You find yourself in a beautiful meadow.

In front of you is a building made of pure crystal.

The crystal shimmers like a rainbow and seems to be changing colour minute by minute.

First it is green, then blue, then indigo, then violet.

You walk towards the crystal building.

The door to the building is green and has two words written upon it which simply say: THE PALACE

You open the green door and walk into the crystal palace.

The palace interior is of such breathtaking beauty. You notice your environment. What does it look like?

You feel so peaceful and so very joyful inside this beautiful crystal palace.

You feel safe.

You feel balanced.

You feel loved and supported.

You feel absolute bliss.

There is a white door in front of you. The white door opens and a beautiful woman steps through. She has long white hair and she is wearing a long white robe with a golden sash tied around it. She wears a crystal necklace around her neck. It is a silver cord with crystals of green, blue, indigo, violet, gold, silver, platinum, magenta and white.

She walks over to you.

"I am Star, the white goddess," she says. "Keeper of the crystal flame."

She hands you a black velvet bag. You take the bag and look inside. You see four crystals. Green, blue, indigo and violet.

"For you to complete the rainbow necklace of memory. Until the next phase."

"The next phase?" you ask. "What do you mean?"

"There will come a time when you will create the royal crystal crown. For now, you have the crystals to complete the rainbow necklace of memory. It will show you the way."

The white goddess smiles at you and then turns and disappears back through the white door.

You look back at the four crystals in your hand. They too each have a hole in them and you thread them upon the cord alongside the other crystals.

You now have seven crystals. Red, orange, yellow, green, blue, indigo and violet.

You put the rainbow necklace of memory around your neck.

As soon as you do this, you find yourself back in the little room standing in front of the red door.

You touch the crystal necklace around your neck to check that it is still there. "Yes, it is still there," you say to yourself. "I can take it with me."

You begin to feel the awareness coming back to your physical body.

You open the red door and walk through.

* * * * *

At this point, allow the awareness to return slowly into each part of your body. You can bring your awareness consciously into each part of your body in turn, by wriggling your toes and fingers, moving your head, or stretching different parts of your body.

When you feel your awareness is fully back into the physical body, you can open your eyes and complete the meditation.

You can place your hands within the namaste prayer position, if you wish to do this; and give thanks to your higher guidance system (the intelligent cosmic consciousness that is 'the matrix') for assisting you with this visual journey within.

If you want to, you can take notes about any thoughts that came to you within the meditation that you feel are significant. Remember to have a pen and notebook next to you before you start, if you feel you will want to make notes.

Meditation

The Mer and the Blue Palace of Atlantis

This particular meditation can be read through, just as with the other meditations, and then followed in an eyes closed or open eyed meditation.

Yet, due to the heavily encoded language of light communications between your conscious self and the matrix, you can also utilise this particular meditation differently.

You can sit comfortably and read this meditation aloud to yourself as if you were reading a story. This works at a deep level to 'pass information' if you will, to the matrix aspect of self (the Source self). The information you are passing is that of activating, accelerating or expanding the crystalline matrix formation that is already taking place within you. Reading this aloud is a 'fast tracking' element, if you will, into the crystalline matrix formation, should you wish to ultilise the story/guided meditation in this way. Happy activations!

* * * * *

As you move into the state of consciousness you know as meditation, imagine, if you will, that you are lying on a sandy beach.

The shining sun creates a warm glow across your body and face, and you feel completely at peace. You feel energised, healed and detoxified by the rays of the sun.

You hear the waves gently lapping on the shore.

As you drift into a wonderful and deeply relaxing sleep, you think to yourself, *What would it be like to swim beneath the ocean and discover its hidden depths?*

You are aware that the last thought you have before sleep is a key into the dream imagery and landscape of the dream experience that follows.

Your last image before falling asleep was that of you discovering the wonder of the water world that is the sea.

As you move into a deep sleep, into the space known as dreamtime, you find yourself moving, in a wave pattern, as a wave pattern and you think to yourself, *Do I have form? Am I physical?*

And as you think these thoughts, you become aware of a body, a physical self, with face, hair, arms, hands and torso.

Yet where there once were legs, you feel this propelling wave force moving you forward through the environmental substance that surrounds you.

After a while of moving through this rhythmic wave pattern, as the wave pattern, you realise it is water you move through and it is water you exist within.

You are swimming through water! And you realise that not only can you breathe in this underwater environment but that you belong here. It is all you have known within this alternate aspect of self, the presentation of your imagination fields of hyperspace merge with the memories and the knowings of that which you know as Lemuria and Atlantis.

You realise the propelling wave force moving you forward, where your legs used to be, is your tail. Your long, strong tail.

Then you know what you are and who you are. You are a creature of the sea, daughter or son of Neptune, guided by Poseidon, known by many in your world as 'mermaids' or 'mermen'. Yet you know that you are part of one of the elemental kingdom groups, known as the 'Mer'.

Memories stir within you as your propel yourself forward through the ocean's pathways. You are one of the Mer. Within the sideways arms of the sacred cross, the horizontal rainbow bridge pathway that moves from left to right, you realise this aspect of self exists within the field of the alternate self.

The Mer of Lemuria, transformed into the priests of Atlantis; you are both of these aspects and your knowing holds the memories of that which came before and that which shall be returned to in the transformed creative unknown.

183

Here you are, here you swim, with the mission of making known the unknown. At this point in your enjoyment of the waters surrounding you, caressing you, comforting you and protecting you, you realise the Mer exists also in the diagonal stream of the matrix fields. There you shall find the seal.

For the ancestral line, moving far, far back within your evolution, you see you were a creature of the waters and before that a being of ether. Swimming within the void of consciousness that is the antimatter representation of all that you know as water.

As these thoughts move through your being and the memories return and take their place as knowings, you see within the distance before you, a beautiful underwater palace.

The blue palace, shining with the bluest of blue ethereal light. This, you know, is the home of the Mer. You have travelled from Lemuria into the blue palace of Atlantis, to access the hidden vault and retrieve your golden blueprints.

"This is my destiny," you say to yourself.

And you happily swim through the underwater golden gates and into the blue palace gardens. Here the fish swim past you, they pay you no mind for you are part of them, they are your family.

The fish possess the brightest of rainbow colours of the like you have never seen in the material, waking world.

You swim into the blue palace and allow the energy, intelligence and love of the blue ray to surround you, cushion you and embrace you.

Here you are safe, here you are sheltered and here you will flourish and nourish yourself at all levels.

The connection with the father Neptune runs in your veins, the connection of the guidance of Poseidon hands you the crown. In your royal awareness, you embrace the memories of all that it means to be Mer.

There before you lies the vault, guarded by three angels with blue-white wings.

They sing to you in the most glorious of tones.

"We, the blue angels of Atlantis do recognise the seal of the Mer that you do carry. You, child of the Royal House of the Galactic Cross, we do allow you access to the vault that is yours alone."

You swim forward and effortlessly open the vault. There, before you, are the golden blueprints that are yours. They belong to you, they are your seal and activate the crystal genetic intelligence that is rightfully yours.

As the golden blueprints merge with all that is you, you feel the duality of the body of the Mer, and of the body of you sleeping peacefully upon the sandy beach.

The angels cast a blue light of guidance for you as you swim back to the ocean pathway, knowing you are merged with the golden blueprints of the crystalline alignment.

The genetic line of the Royal House of the Galactic Cross rises again upon Gaia in all that is you, child of the stars. You claim your inheritance and honour your heritage with the merging of the blue ray and the golden blueprints within.

As you swim forward, gliding through the water, ocean substance of life force, you become aware of the self that lays upon the sandy beach, basking in the light of the sun.

Once again you are lying upon the sandy beach, hearing the waves lapping upon the shore.

You smile to yourself for you know you have experienced the journey of the Mer, from Lemuria to Atlantis and reclaimed the golden blueprints of the crystalline alignment.

You are aware now of your actual physical body, in meditation. As your awareness moves into the physical body, you are aware of the memories you have uncovered and the codes that have been set in place.

* * * * *

At this point, allow the awareness to return slowly into each part of your body. You can bring your awareness consciously into each part of your body in turn, by wriggling your toes and fingers, moving your head, or stretching different parts of your body.

When you feel your awareness is fully back into the physical body, you can open your eyes and complete the meditation.

You can place your hands within the namaste prayer position, if you wish to do this; and give thanks to your higher guidance system (the intelligent cosmic consciousness that is 'the matrix') for assisting you with this visual journey within.

If you want to, you can take notes about any thoughts that came to you within the meditation that you feel are significant. Remember to have a pen and notebook next to you before you start, if you feel you will want to make notes.

Meditation

Architecture of Light (Your Temple)

Within your meditation, visualise, if you will, the space around you.

You find that you are in a temple.

You are sat, cross-legged, on a red rug.

Before you stands a beautiful woman with long, flowing, dark hair.

"Welcome to the Temple of Divinity," she says. "It is time for you to change the hyperspace landscape around you."

"The Temple of Divinity is your divine template."

"The Temple is the template."

As soon as the beautiful woman speaks the words, "The Temple is the template," then the landscape around you begins to transform.

You find yourself in a space. The hyperspace visuals around you are that of geometry, light and colour.

You are stood upright with your arms outstretched within this visual field.

Your feet are firmly rooted upon a bed of stars.

Your reconstruction of the divine architecture of the matrix, your temple, your template, begins to take form.

From above, descending from the overworld dimensions, a vertical pillar of light moves down, through your crown chakra, moving down through each chakra in turn and down through the root chakra, continuing into the underworld dimensions.

A vertical pillar of light moves upwards from the underworld dimensions through your root chakra, moving upwards through each chakra and up through the crown chakra into the cosmos above and the overworld dimensions.

The pillar of light coming down from the cosmos is a silver white light.

You are aware that you are being 'anointed' with the platinum ray and the diamond light.

The pillar of light moving upwards from the root chakra is a golden white light.

You are aware that you are being 'initiated' by the golden ray and the diamond light.

You are aware that the diamond light is the template for ascension and the return to the 'Christos Sphere', the place we know as 'Krysta'.

From your left to your right, a horizontal energy vortex as a 'horizontal light filament' moves through you and intersects with the vertical pillar at your solar plexus chakra point.

This 'horizontal rainbow bridge pathway', containing the rainbow light codes, merges with the pillar of light at your solar plexus.

You feel this intersection of merging vertical and horizontal streams as a convergence point of energy. You feel this within the solar plexus as a 'ball of energy'. This energy sphere begins to rotate in an anticlockwise direction.

The rainbow/diamond ray light merge as a spinning sphere expands upwards to connect with your heart chakra and then begins to spin in a clockwise direction.

The horizontal rainbow energy vortex light stream moves from behind you, through the solar plexus and heart chakra intersection point and moves out in front of you stretching into infinity.

You now stand within the sacred cross, as the sacred cross.

Your solar plexus, heart centre at the pivot point connects this sacred cross constructed of diamond and rainbow light codes into your conscious awareness.

An emerald light moves in diagonally from your left, intersecting at your solar plexus heart centre convergence point. The pivot point, zero point field.

A magenta light moves in diagonally from the right, intersecting at your solar plexus heart centre convergence point. The pivot point, zero point field.

That which is the white wheel, the light wheel, constructed of diamond light codes, rainbow light codes and the transformative lovelight/lightlove streams of the emerald and magenta rays is constructed around you as your Temple of Divinity.

This is your 'starseed template' and is your personal 'divine architecture'.

The individual chakra points begin to join with the diamond light of the vertical pillar.

The individual chakra points join and merge as one with the rainbow light of the horizontal pathway.

The individual chakra points join and merge as one with the emerald and magenta light ray streams.

Here, within this wheel, the rainbow Mer-Ka-Bah, your temple/template, you know you activate the codes and water the seeds of the crystalline blueprint.

The light of the Christos and the city of Krysta, the 'emerald crystal city' is now all that you see, all that you hold and all that you are.

The past/future rainbow bridge merges with the crystalline template and becomes one moment, one time and one space.

The alternate/parallel/quantum streams of possibility and probability, within the horizontal rainbow bridge pathway, that which we also call the 'sideways arm of the cross', merge with the crystalline template and become one integrated, whole self within the wholistic grid, Mer-Ka-Bah wheel.

The paternal ancestral diagonal magenta light lines and the maternal ancestral diagonal emerald light lines merge with the crystalline template and bring all into the now, the zero point field, within all that is you, resolving the repeating karmic patterns within those fields and moving you into the spin of true multidimensionality.

As you stand within your architecture of light, your Temple of Divinity in the Emerald City of Krysta, you also stand within the Christ light, Christ consciousness, Christos Sphere.

This is the formation for the crystal body, rainbow body, celestial body, diamond light body. This is the place where the twelve divide and multiply and you stand within the grid of the 144,000 warriors of light.

You remain within this space for a while, holding the light formations of your divine architecture as you contemplate the new awareness and the epiphanies that move into your grid. You allow the activation of the higher heart space and the crystallised energy body, rainbow chakra alignment.

You embrace the thoughts, visuals, sounds, words, symbols, colours and emotions as they come to you within the safe zone, the zero point, the hidden vault. You are enshrouded, anointed and initiated into the knowings of the Gaia grid, galactic grid, celestial, hermetic seal.

The expansion and activation is seeded and it flourishes in the sacred space of your divine architecture.

You take a while in perfect merged unity and contemplation as you relax into the Source space that is yours and is you.

After a while, you allow your thoughts to return to the physical plane.

You leave your crystallised Temple of Divinity intact, knowing you can return to this unified alchemical merge, crystalline template activation any time you so choose.

You begin to feel the dualistic sensations of the rainbow self with the aspect of self sitting in the Temple of Divinity upon the red rug.

As soon as you have that thought, you find yourself sitting on the red rug within the Temple of Divinity with the beautiful dark-haired woman standing before you.

"I am Aurora," she says. "I am the keeper of the Emerald City of Krysta."

You smile at the beautiful goddess Aurora.

"Now this place is yours. Now you truly hold the unified, quantum field of creation within your heart. Now you are the rainbow and you hold the activated crystalline formation."

Yes... you think to yourself. You allow Aurora's words to resonate within you. *Yes, I do hold the unified quantum field of creation within my heart and I am the crystalline formation. This is my starseed template, my divine architecture of Mer-Ka-Bah light.*

Aurora waves and smiles at you as she begins to fade.

Your awareness starts to returns to your third dimensional physical body.

You are now fully centred and grounded within the physical body in the third dimension of reality, yet you continue to hold the crystalline template of activation.

* * * * *

At this point, allow the awareness to return slowly into each part of your body. You can bring your awareness consciously into each part of your body in turn, by wriggling your toes and fingers, moving your head, or stretching different parts of your body.

When you feel your awareness is fully back into the physical body, you can open your eyes and complete the meditation.

You can place your hands within the namaste prayer position, if you wish to do this; and give thanks to your higher guidance system (the intelligent cosmic consciousness that is 'the matrix') for assisting you with this visual journey within.

If you want to, you can take notes about any thoughts that came to you within the meditation that you feel are significant. Remember to have a pen and notebook next to you before you start, if you feel you will want to make notes.

Enjoy this book?

Check out magentapixie.com

Vast video archive of Magenta Pixie's messages
Downloadable guided meditations
Interviews, lectures, free stuff and more!

Also by Magenta Pixie...
available in print and Kindle edition

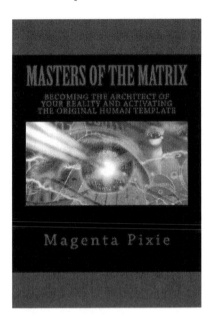

Masters of the Matrix: Becoming the Architect of Your Reality and Activating the Original Human Template

"An extraordinary contribution to Humanity and the Great Shift."

"A Priceless Gift... This is THE most helpful book I have come across yet on my journey... It's a bible."

"Sensational! This book is full of high voltage encoded information... One of the Best books available explaining the multidimensional perspective."

- Amazon customer reviews

Printed in Poland
by Amazon Fulfillment
Poland Sp. z o.o., Wrocław